AF521659

ALSO BY PAUL BAILEY

Fiction

For Time and All Eternity

For This My Glory

Type High

Deliver Me From Eva

The Gray Saint

Song Everlasting

The Claws of the Hawk

Ghost Dance Messiah

History and Biography

The Armies of God (the Little Known Story of the Mormon Militia on the American Frontier)

Sam Brannan and the California Mormons

Fabulous Farmer (the Story of Walter Knott and His Berry Farm)—with Roger Holmes

Walkara, Hawk of the Mountains

Wovoka, the Indian Messiah

Grandpa Was a Polygamist

Jacob Hamblin, Buckskin Apostle

City in the Sun (the Japanese Concentration Camp at Poston, Arizona)

Concentration Camp U.S.A.

Polygamy Was Better Than Monotony

Those Kings and Queens of Old Hawaii

Editor and Compiler of

The Mormons In California
(Pioneer Journal of William Glover)

HOLY SMOKE

A Dissertation on the Utah War

Great West Indian Series, Vol. 44

HOLY SMOKE

A Dissertation on the Utah War

by Paul Bailey

WESTERNLORE BOOKS . . . 1978 . . . LOS ANGELES, CALIF.

©

COPYRIGHT 1978
BY PAUL BAILEY
All Rights Reserved

Library of Congress Catalog No. 77-088721
ISBN No. 0-87026-037-5

PRINTED IN THE UNITED STATES OF AMERICA BY WESTERNLORE PRESS

TABLE OF CONTENTS

TABLE OF ILLUSTRATIONS

I

"Those rights so dearly purchased . . ."

CHILDHOOD recollection of this writer is haunted by vivid remembrance of his grandmother on the maternal side, an intelligent and lively old Mormon lady, who tenderly jogged him on her knee to such folk tunes as

"When Johnston's Army comes,
We'll drown 'em in the lake,
  And leave their bones
  To bleach upon the sand!
On the sand!"

Johnston's Army, even in this writer's early Utah years, was a menace practically drowned in obscurity. It continued, however, to possess a certain vivid recollection to Grandma. But to her grandson, and to the world's grandsons, this weird chapter of American history with all its interplay of comic and tragic incidents, has bleached its bones for a long and unheeded time.

And in digging up the forgotten bones of the "Utah War" one encounters at every turn the ubiquitous ghost of

Thomas Leiper Kane — always a little aloof from the shades of the commanders of the Utah Expedition, and Brigham Young's Mormons who bitterly resisted them — but ever present.

Aside from the military operations to put down the Mormon "rebellion" of 1857 — a rebellion which Utah Mormons insist was dreamed up in the minds of their adversaries — there were a number of side dramas, from operatic stage-strutting to the bloody violence and explosive curtain-calls which wiped a president out of the White House, overturned a political dynasty, built freighting monopolies, affected drastically the course of the Civil War to immediately follow, and re-channeled the very course of history pertaining to America's West. And yet, without the still inexplicable humanitarian and sacrificial acts of that one man — Thomas Leiper Kane — a drama of far greater import—one in which blood and horror would have intermingled, and one in which American people must of necessity have accepted forever to their shame — was so narrowly averted as to border on the miraculous.

The great religious migration of the Mormon people from Illinois to Great Salt Lake Valley in 1847 is still a classic study in mob violence and mass hysteria. That social pressure could grow into intensity sufficient to expel an entire commonwealth from a land of its pioneering is almost incredible unless one probes the underlying causes of the hates and suspicions feeding strength to the mass-force which brought about this expulsion. No less curious is the national and political hysteria which ten years later induced President James B. Buchanan and the Congress of the United States to dispatch an army almost equal in size to that ragged Mormon populace who, by this time, had found peace and the beginning of prosperity in the arid and unwanted lands of the Great Basin.

Who was wrong and who was right in the American incident of the "Utah War" is a matter best left to time and evidence. What is of concern is the marshaling of facts, the scrutiny of motives, and reconstructing a frame to this lively and entertaining segment of history.

Mormons today have gained a respectability among their American neighbors which would have amazed their murdered prophet, Joseph Smith, or their harassed leader, Brigham Young. The peace which now sheds beneficence and warmth over "Zion" is a satisfaction never experienced by the founders and early converts to the Church of Jesus Christ of Latter-day Saints in its turbulent beginnings.

In those days, under the withering blasts of press and pulpit, under the constant threat of physical harm, it took a dogged courage to stand up and be counted as an adherent to this despised sect. A Mormon in the days of the Nauvoo expulsion or Johnston's Army was just about as popular as a Palestinian terrorist in today's news. Little wonder that Mormons still pay homage to those few courageous "Gentiles" like Colonel Alexander Doniphan, Colonel Philip St. George Cooke, and Colonel Thomas L. Kane, who once raised voices in defense of their rights as Americans and as humans.

The Mormon Prophet himself had set precedents for his people. "Those rights so dearly purchased shall not be disgracefully trodden under foot by lawless marauders without a noble effort on our part to sustain our liberties. . . ."[1]

[1]Smith, Joseph (B. H. Roberts ed.), *History of the Church*, Period I, Vol. VI, pp. 497-498.

GREAT SALT LAKE VALLEY—JULY 1847
As the Mormons First Saw It

—From Whitney's *History of Utah.*

II
Territorial Travail

By 1857, the year of hostilities, the Latter-day Saints had builded their Zion in the Rocky Mountains; had planted their colonies from the Great Salt Lake to the Pacific Coast; had in great measure "made the desert blossom as the rose." In a forbidding land, a land unclaimed and unwanted by other men, the Saints had erected a powerful and cohesive commonwealth.

And yet all this was only ten years from the time their revered prophet, Joseph Smith, had been murdered by rioting mobs in Carthage, Illinois, and the despised sect literally ousted from the then borders of the United States. One decade only had passed since their epic migration westward had commenced.

By now Zion was vastly more than just a Mormon dream of freedom from mob-rule and persecution. In ten years, under the strange industry of these people, Utah had risen from sagebrush prairie to one of the largest and most promising of American territories, with yearly petitions for its admission into the Union as one of the States. It had become the most important center of population between the Missouri River and California in that immense land area wrested from Mexico at the conclusion of the Mexican War.

Brigham Young was Utah Territory's governor, by Mormon desire and governmental appointment. An unorthodox type of Christianity, including polygamous marriages, was being advocated and openly practiced by members of the sect. And, because of the insularity and the unconventional nature of Mormonism itself, there was no dearth of strange and curious stories coming out of Utah.

By 1857 facts and fancies had become so embellished by lurid tales and fertile imaginings that practically every crusading editor and sin-conscious divine would have considered himself remiss in duty not to have expounded publicly on the "Mormon Menace." No one-hundred-percent American of 1857 doubted for a moment that something must be done about Mormons. The only question seems to have been which retributive measure might be most effective in dealing with the "heretical brigands" who were fast populating the west with converts and offspring.

In the tenth year after the Saints had entered Salt Lake Valley, tension had mounted to the explosion point. Oddly, it was Mormons themselves who put torch to the blast.

ESTABLISHMENT OF CIVIL GOVERNMENT

One of the first tasks attempted by the Mormons on their arrival in the Valley of the Great Salt Lake was the setting up of a workable form of civil government, with courts, magistrates—and the claimed jurisdiction of a state comprising a slice of the west so immense as to include a part of Southern California. This state, which

Mormons named Deseret,[1] was eventually whittled down by the American government to the Territory of Utah, which even in abbreviated form was considerably larger than the present state of that name.

Despite much which has been published to the contrary, Mormons showed none of the inclination to set up a separate nation or strictly Mormon government in the Great Basin of which they so often have been accused. On the contrary, they raised the flag of the United States in Salt Lake Valley while it was yet Mexican territory, months before United States authority was extended over it.[2] All this, too, while the Saints, fresh from the Illinois expulsion, still smarted under the injustices so maliciously dealt them, and the general apathy of the government toward their destitute and unhappy lot or their petitions for redress of the wrongs dealt them by their fellow citizens.

Their proposed "State of Deseret," while apparently germinating in the minds of the Saints and their leaders from their first arrival in the Valley, did not take form and substance until February of 1849, nearly two years after their entry, and only after the government itself had been willfully negligent in providing any form of governmental control over the vast area ceded to it from Mexico. In that month came a "Call for a Convention to Form Civil Government in the Great Basin" to "all the citizens of that portion of Upper California lying east of the Sierra

[1]"And they did also carry with them *deseret*, which, by interpretation, is a honey bee."—*Book of Mormon*, p. 480, ch. 2, verse 3. The great seal of the State of Utah is the beehive.

[2]See Roberts, B. H., *Comprehensive History of the Church of Jesus Christ of Latter-day Saints*, vol. III, p. 275. The flag was raised sometime in October of 1847, on a staff *within the fort*, and not atop Ensign Peak, as often claimed by the Mormon people.

Nevada Mountains."[3] Convention date was set for March 6 of that year at Great Salt Lake City.

Out of it came a constitution for a provisional state government which, in general form, followed the pattern of the majority of state constitutions then operative. It is interesting that complete religious freedom for all sects was emphatically affirmed.[4] Elections were held immediately following the convention, with a select panel of Mormon officials as candidates. Brigham Young appears to have been unanimous choice for governor.

The constitutional convention in memorializing Congress for admittance into the Union of their proposed State of Deseret apparently watered down their request with an "if" or two. "Your memorialists therefore ask your honorable body to favorably consider their interests; and, if consistent with the Constitution and usages of the federal government, that the Constitution accompanying this memorial be ratified, and that the 'State of Deseret' be admitted into the Union on an equal footing with other states, or such other form of civil government as your wisdom and magnanimity may award to the people of Deseret. And, upon the adoption of any form of government here, that their delegates be received, and their interests properly and faithfully represented, in the congress of the United States . . ."[5]

THE UNFORTUNATE ALTERNATIVE

As though convinced their application for statehood would be denied them, and without even waiting for a reply from Congress as to the memorial, a month later Dr. John M. Bernhisel was on his way east with a petition for a

[3]*History of Brigham Young, Ms.*, for 1849, entry 1st Feb., p. 3. Quoted also in Roberts, *Comprehensive History*, vol. III, pp. 422-423.

[4]Article iii, *Constitution, "State of Deseret,"* sec. 2.

[5]*Millennial Star*, vol. XII, p. 24. Quoted also in Roberts, *Comprehensive History*, vol. III, pp. 428-429.

territorial form of government, signed not only by Brigham Young and the leaders, but by 2,270 residents of the Valley.[6] Bernhisel was instructed to call upon Colonel Thomas L. Kane, whose friendship and good offices had previously served the Mormons well. In the matter of gaining territorial status, Kane, for the second time, was to be given complete power of attorney in negotiating for Mormon interests. In Bernhisel's portfolio was also a letter of introduction to Senator Stephen A. Douglas, in the hope his once magnanimous attitude toward the Saints would again prevail, and that he would assist them through the political maze at Washington.

While the boundaries of Deseret, whether state or territory, encircled a generous slice of the North American continent, it is the only point at which Congress or the American people had a right to criticize the Mormons on their petition for some sort of government. Certainly neither belligerence nor high-handedness is evident in their complaisant request for practically any form of government which the "wisdom or magnanimity" of Congress might "award to the people of 'Deseret'."

Apostle Wilford Woodruff joined Bernhisel in the interview with Thomas L. Kane at Philadelphia regarding the matter, and received from the young attorney some pertinent and prophetical advice. "You are better off without any government from the hands of Congress than with a territorial government," Kane emphatically declared. "The political intrigues of government officers will be against you. You can govern yourselves better than they can govern you. I would prefer to see you withdraw the bill, rather than to have a territorial government, for if you are defeated in the state government,

[6]Roberts, *Comprehensive History*, vol. III, p. 420.

you can fall back upon it again another session, if you have not a territorial government; but if you have, you cannot apply for a state government for a number of years.

". . . You do not want corrupt political men from Washington strutting around you, with military epaulettes and dress, who will speculate out of you all they can. They will also control the Indian agency, and Land agency, and will conflict with your calculations in a great measure. You have a government now—the provisional state government of Deseret already in existence—which is firm and powerful, and you are under no obligations to the United States.

"If you have a state government," Kane argued, "men may come along and say, 'I am judge,' 'I am colonel,' 'I am governor,' you can whistle and ask no odds of them. But while you have a territorial government you cannot do it. And then there are so many intrigues to make political parties among you, the first thing you know, a strong political party is rising up in your midst, selfish, and against your interests."[7]

Apparently Bernhisel took Kane's advice seriously, refused to petition Congress for territorial status, and became immediately active in Washington in furthering the cause of the "State of Deseret" before both congressional houses. A labor already foredoomed to failure.

In the meantime, back in Salt Lake Valley, Deseret's state leaders had been sworn into office at a meeting of the general assembly on July 2, 1849. Almon W. Babbitt was elected delegate and representative to Congress; the memorial to Congress already in the hands of Bernhisel, Woodruff and Kane was "adopted." With printed and

[7]Roberts, *Comprehensive History,* vol. III, p. 432. Recorded *extenso* in *History of Brigham Young, Ms.,* 1849, pp. 161-164.

certified copies of both this and the constitution of the provisional state, Babbitt followed Bernhisel to Washington.

STATEHOOD DENIED

Babbitt never came remotely near a seat in Congress. Washington was chilly toward the Mormon dream of statehood. The Mormon delegates, convinced of the wisdom of Kane's advice in regard to territorial status, soft-pedaled all prayers to Congress on that phase of their memorial. But in their hopes for genuine statehood they met complete and final defeat.

On September 9, 1849 an act creating the Territory of Utah became a law.[8] The new territory's boundaries were whittled down to a size Congress considered more appropriate. Wishes of the Mormon people as to name, geographical area, and self-government were entirely ignored.

Senator Douglas, on December 27, 1849, formally but tardily submitted the Mormon petition for statehood to the same Congress. But Washington's august lawmakers were neither in mood to properly act on the memorial, nor to seat Deseret's delegate. Nearly fifty years must pass before this far west commonwealth was to become a sister member of the American states. In the meantime the worst of Colonel Kane's predictions were to come true, and Utah was to reap a whirlwind from the furies thus engendered.

[8] *Organic Act Creating the Territory of Utah*, sec. i.

GREAT SALT LAKE CITY IN 1853

III
Kane, the Tireless Advocate

Colonel Kane's advice and interview relative to Mormon statehood was not the first efforts the young lawyer had made in behalf of the strange sect with which he held continuing sympathy. "It appears from this interview," says B. H. Roberts, "that Colonel Kane had presented even an earlier petition for territorial government for the Salt Lake colonists; and that this petition was tentatively presented in the closing months of President Polk's administration; and then withdrawn because Colonel Kane could not be sure that territorial officers from among the colonists would be appointed, but men from the east who would not be in sympathy with them; from which circumstances he foresaw great difficulties would arise—and they did afterwards arise—and hence he withdrew the petition he had presented."[1]

In regard to that earlier and aborted effort toward territorial status, Kane explained to Bernhisel and Woodruff, "I applied, according to the wish of President Young, for a

[1]Roberts, *Comprehensive History*, vol. III, p. 432.

territorial government. I had my last sad and painful interview with President Polk. I found he did not feel disposed to favor your people, and he had his men of his own stamp picked out to serve as governor and other officers, who would have oppressed you or injured you in any way to fill their own pockets. He would not appoint men from among yourselves, and I saw it absolutely necessary that you should have officers of your own people to govern you, or you were better without any government. I had to use my own discretion, and I withdrew the petition."[2]

Even prior to this there are a number of incidents where Kane acted as liaison between the Mormon people and their suspicious and often openly hostile government. Never did Kane show inclination to become a Mormon, but always was he vigorous in their defense. The reasons for his championing of so unpopular a cause must of necessity be searched out of the record itself. Towns, counties, schools throughout Utah have been named in reverent honor of this young soldier and barrister who talked Mormon and remained Gentile. For a time, Council Bluffs, Iowa, was actually renamed "Kanesville" in his honor by the grateful and remembering Saints. From either the Mormon eulogistic standpoint, or the broad principles of humanitarianism and love of simple justice, Thomas Leiper Kane stands as an American phenomenon.

He was the son of a prominent federal judge, John Kintzing Kane, and brother to Elisha Kent Kane, the great Arctic explorer. He was born January 27, 1822 in Philadelphia, where he completed his schooling and gained his officerial commission. He spent considerable time in Europe while a young man, and in those impres-

[2]*Ibid.*, p. 445.

sionable years became closely acquainted with the renowned French philosopher, Auguste Comte. The mark of Comte appears throughout Kane's life.

In 1864 young Kane was admitted to the bar, and began his career as a junior counsel in his father's Philadelphia office. In that same year came his first experience with the Mormons. Elder Jesse Little was on his way to Washington to plead sufferance and aid for the thousands of destitute Latter-day Saints then being driven from Illinois into the bleakly winterbound and inhospitable west. Specifically, Elder Little hoped that the government might commission these people to build forts and blockhouses on the route to Oregon, compensation for the services to be used to feed the hungry Saints then temporarily encamped on the Iowa banks of the Missouri, and to assist their removal as a people to the far west.

SOJOURN WITH THE SAINTS

Kane was so moved by Little's revealment of the tragic plight of these refugees that he immediately started west to ascertain the facts for himself. If the tales of Mormon destitution and American brutality toward them were true, he was resolved to lend what effort he could in their behalf.

His 1846 journey into the west, where he visited the empty and ghostlike Mormon city of Nauvoo, in Illinois, and rode horseback across the Iowa prairie to the fever and hunger infested Mormon camps, filled him with pity and horror. His written accounts of what he saw on that journey are undoubtedly the most lucid non-Mormon descriptives of those turbulent and tragic years.

". . . Upon what is called the big prairie over which their course lay and on which nothing above the grass breaks the free course of the biting winds from the North and the great lakes, wood is often difficult to obtain and the comfort of a campfire not to be had. It will not be wondered at then, that the sufferings of this body gave them, to use their own phrase, a very good idea of those exiles traveling to Siberia . . . The suffering from cold may be imagined. If nothing else, the less vigorous constitutions were dangerously frost-bitten, while many of the stoutest men were by the same visitation rendered lame and unable to walk. The animals of draught employed suffered no less; they of course were without shelter and were without wholesome food; as the farmers of Iowa refused to sell their corn to Mormons unless at such exorbitant prices as they were unable to pay . . . Add to this an insufficient provision of food was made for the human beings also on the expedition and it will be seen that there was enough in such extremity to terrify the bravest of them . . .

". . . It was at this time that most sickness prevailed. The most hearty went about bent with rheumatism and the old persons and children died in greater numbers than during the coldest of the winter and what was worse the women who had been the most cheerful & heroic & who had helped sustain the courage of the stoutest . . ."[3]

Kane found that the Illinois "antis" had violated "their last solemn agreement as to allowing Mormons peaceable and leisurely exodus from their lands and cities. Affairs had been hurried up by liberal use of powder and ball. Nauvoo, their "city beautiful" had been sacked and the great temple despoiled, and eager citizens had blandly appropriated all farms, homes and livestock the unfortunate Saints had been unable to sell or convert into traveling necessities.

[3]Kane, Thomas Leiper, *A Friend of the Mormons,* the Private Papers and Diary of Thomas Leiper Kane, edited by Oscar Osburn Winther, pp. 2-3

The man from Philadelphia arrived in time to see the Mormons struggling across Iowa in immense numbers; he witnessed the beginnings of the amazing system of organization for common good which was forged out of their adversity. Their cheerfulness and courage under hardship won his unbounded respect. He found immense tracts of land at Garden Grove and Mount Pisgah being plowed and put under cultivation, that those who followed might reap and eat. By July 11 he was at the farthest Mormon outposts on the banks of the Missouri River, and had met and became favorably acquainted with Brigham Young and the other hardy leaders of the great exodus.

THE MORMON BATTALION IS BORN

His arrival had been preceded by that of Captain James Allen, U.S. Army, who had surprised the Mormons with his unexpected arrival for the purpose of recruiting a Battalion for service in the war with Mexico.[4] The letter which Allen had brought north from Fort Leavenworth, written by Colonel Stephen W. Kearny and giving authority and instruction for the mustering in of a Mormon army, was the first intimation Brigham Young had of the trend of Washington conversations between Little, Kane, Polk, and government officialdom.

"There was apparently some reluctance among the people to respond to this unexpected call, and it required

[4] "Captain James Allen of the United States Army arrived at Mount Pisgah on the 26th of June, accompanied by three dragoons. The camp was momentarily thrown into great excitement by this event, and the cry ran throughout the camp—'*The United States troops are upon us! The United States troops are upon us!*' The excitement and the cry of alarm rose from remembrance of the reported intention of the federal government before the Saints began leaving Nauvoo, to prevent the movement to the west by the employment, if necessary, of the United States troops, as falsely reported by Governor Ford . . ."—Roberts, *Comprehensive History,* vol. III, p. 64.

BRIGHAM YOUNG
From a Daguerrotype Taken in 1855

some persuasion to dispel it," says Roberts.[5] The timely arrival of the saddle-weary Kane at the Council Bluffs camp, gave the necessary persuasion to completion of the project. Kane immediately met with Brigham Young and the leaders, explained the reasons for the unexpected call, and the advantages which could be expected from so unmistakable a proof of loyalty to the United States Government. He explained Elder Little's promotion of the plan in Washington, and with the sudden and fortuitous arrival of Jesse Little himself, the recruitment went on with alacrity and dispatch.

On July 20, 1846 the Mormon Battalion, under Allen's command, started its march southward toward Fort Leavenworth. This draining of five hundred ablest men from the "camps of Israel," together with desperately needed wagons and livestock, unfortunately, proved the final crippling blow to Mormon plans to move farther westward in the summer of 1846. While the Mormon Battalion was making its own peculiar history in the Mexican War, the families it left behind at Council Bluffs, Pisgah and Garden Grove, were gathered with all the other destitute Saints into winter quarters on the west bank of the Missouri.

All was not sacrifice, however. In promptly acceding to the call for volunteers, the homeless Mormons carved out a gain for themselves which the canny Brigham was quick to see. The almost simultaneous appearance of Kane, Allen and Little in behalf of the projected army occurred during the very lowest ebb of Mormon fortunes. The season was late—the year had been whittled away by endless problems incident to organizing one of the great mass migrations of history. Disease and hunger stalked

[5]*Ibid.*, Vol. III, p. 80

the clotted roadways of Iowa and the "camps of Israel" between the Missouri and the Mississippi. Brigham's hopes of at least reaching Grand Island before winter set in were being brought to naught by the insuperable demands made upon him by his host of nearly ten thousand sick and destitute Saints. Money for supplies had long since been exhausted. Though some of the Mormon men had found employment among their hostile neighbors of Iowa and Missouri, the trickle of cash from this source would not begin to put bread in the mouths of the thousands now clawing the leader for desperately needed help and direction. Winter quarters already had been decided upon, but Brigham Young was convinced that only a miracle could now save his people.

He had petitioned the United States Government for help in the crisis, but the plea had fallen on cold hearts and deaf ears. He had begged the President and Congress to send someone to impartially investigate the rape of Nauvoo and the expulsion of his people. Only Thomas L. Kane—at his own expense, and bidden by his own humanitarian impulses—had made the journey or spoken out in their defense. Brigham Young had commissioned Jesse C. Little to offer Mormon manpower in building blockhouses and forts on the route to Oregon, in return for aid in moving the Saints westward. Out of that final overture had come the Mormon Battalion.

If this were the miracle, it came as an odd and unexpected sort of one to the harassed Brigham. But in that capacity he made it serve. The enlistees unselfishly assigned their meager pay as foot soldiers, and even their clothing allowances, to the benefit of the destitute Saints in the "camps of Israel." Mormon messengers were sent to intercept the Battalion at Leavenworth, Santa Fe, and even California to collect the desperately needed cash as it was issued out in pay. Aside from the fact that five hundred Mormon men went west at government expense—under their own motive power—the recruiting of the Battalion saved the Mormon people from outright starvation and almost certain disaster.

In lending willing aid to its recruitment Brigham Young was doubtless seeing all things in mind's eye.[6] "Although we have been inhumanly and barbarously dealt with by the surrounding country where we dwelt, yet the president of the United States is favorably disposed to us. He has sent out orders to have five hundred of our brethren employed in an expedition that was fitting out against California, with orders for them to be employed for one year, and then be discharged in California, and to have their arms and implements of war given to them at the expiration of the term, and as there is no prospect of any opposition, it amounts to the same as paying them for going to the place where they were destined to go without."[7]

"VIOLENT BILIOUS FEVER"

But if Colonel Kane had plans of accompanying the Battalion to California, either in officerial capacity or as interested observer, he was destined to disappointment.

[6]"But in the midst of this we were cheered with the presence of our friend, Mr. Little, of New Hampshire, who assures us of the personal friendship of the president, in the act before us; and this assurance, though not doubted by us in the least, was soon made doubly sure by the testimony of Colonel Kane, of Philadelphia, whose presence in our midst, and the ardor with which he has espoused the cause of a persecuted and suffering people, and the testimony he has borne of your excellency's kind feelings, have kindled up a spark in our hearts which had been well nigh extinguished . . . love of a country, or ruler, from whom previously we had received but little save neglect or persecution."—Letter and resolution to Pres. James K. Polk from Pres. Brigham Young and the Council of the Twelve. *History of Brigham Young, Ms.*, 1846, bk. 2, pp. 137-138.

[7]*Millennial Star*, vol. VIII, p. 117.

It would be Colonel Philip St. George Cooke who finally would lead the Mormon troops west.

On Kane's arrival at the Mormon camp he was ill, remaining so to the extent he was unable to publicly occupy the speaker's stand in its tenderance to him during the enlistment rallies.[8] His condition grew no better as the Battalion marched southward and he remained in friendly care of the Saints. By August 10 his condition had grown so serious that Brigham Young dispatched an express rider southward to Fort Leavenworth with an urgent appeal for medical help.

> The council of the church of Jesus Christ of Latter Day Saints writes you at this time, at the special request of Col. Thomas L. Kane, of Philadelphia, now lying dangerously ill at our camp . . .
>
> Col. Kane is unable to use his pen, and, being afflicted, as he supposes, with a nervous, billious fever, is very desirous of seeing Dr. Londerson immediately, with such medicine as he may deem necessary, and will not impede his progress on the journey . . .
>
> Col. Kane has deposited with us all his available funds at this moment, to wit, $100. Bank of Mo. and a note of bond, *good* $30, as surety for the expenses of the medical officer whom you may send in attendance, and contingent expenses of the ride; but should the expenses be much more, we are assured by Col. Kane that nothing will be wanting as soon as his draft can be answered . . .
>
> There are also other high and important considerations connected with Col. Kane's visit to this place, and reasons of a peculiar nature, which we fully understand but not necessary to mention here, why we, as friends of the Col. would urge the immediate attendance of Dr. Londerson, with whom Col. Kane rode to Table Creek, and is personally acquainted, or, if that be impracticable, some adviser whom you may select; and we cannot too strongly urge a speedy and prompt action on your part, and that of your adviser, by every consideration that binds

[8]Golder, Frank A., *The March of the Mormon Battalion*, p. 121.

noble souls to each other, and tends to alleviate the great sum of human misery.

We shall dispatch this by express, enjoining a change of horses, and full speed.[9]

Conditions at Leavenworth, due to the rapid movement of troops westward, were such that Dr. Londerson could not reach Colonel Kane immediately, in spite of the urgency of the plea. Another physician was found nearer the Mormon camp, a Dr. H. J. W. Edes, from Weston, Missouri. "My opinion is that the disease of Colonel Thomas L. Kane has been the violent Bilious Fever of this region; connecting itself seriously with the Nervous System," was the written diagnosis of Dr. Edes. "It is after the disappearance of this malady that an Intermittent Fever has supervened."

The physician apparently was cognizant that Kane, even though bedfast in a Mormon camp, was in solicitous and friendly care. "From my knowledge of the necessity of careful nursing . . . from Colonel Kane's unmeasured assurances to me; and from what I myself have observed during my visit to this place, I have no hesitation in testifying to the devoted care and kindness with which he has been treated, by his friends the Mormon People. Throughout this camp, where I observe a spirit of harmony and a habit of good order—wonderful in so large an assemblage of people, I find that prevails towards him the warmest and most cordial benevolence of feeling."[10]

Kane never forgot the Mormons nor their "benevolence of feeling" toward him. On his return east he entered into a vigorous defense of the homeless Saints, by

[9]Kane, Thomas L., and Oscar Winther, ed., *A Friend of the Mormons*, the private papers and diaries of Thomas L. Kane, pp. 21-22.

[10]*Ibid.*, p. 23.

writings, by lectures, and every other means at his command. His bold stand never diminished during the hectic decade to follow. With gratitude the Mormon people accepted him as their voice among the Gentiles during these years which established their commonwealth in the Valley of the Great Salt Lake.

Kane pleaded their cause before presidents and congress. He wrote constantly of Mormon worthiness, and the right of the sect to exist amidst hostility. And, when America and the world finally turned full venom upon the Saints, and they stood publicly accused as seditious, traitorous, and in open rebellion against the very nation they owed allegiance, Kane's pro-Mormon stand never paused nor waivered. The great test, however, when this friendly Gentile's courage and concern would be balanced against good judgment and political disaster, was yet to come. It was to be a dramatic measure of an historic friendship.

IV

The Political Appointees

THE UTAH hostilities of 1857-58, whether given in Mormon and Gentile terms as "The Utah War," "Echo Canyon War, "Buchanan's Blunder," or "The Mormon War," has as many diverse beginnings as it has titles. In official government reports the affair is usually referred to as "The Utah Expedition" and military documents simply label it "The Army for Utah," but there can be no oversimplification of its causes. They go back almost to the day the first Mormon plow bit into the arid soil of Salt Lake Valley.

"The 'war,' if so it may be designated, was waged on the part of the general government for the maintenance of the supremacy of the federal authority in the territory of Utah, which Buchanan's administration had been led to believe, or feigned to believe, was questioned in Utah; and against which, it was also led to believe . . . a substantial rebellion existed. On the part of the Latter-day Saints, then constituting practically the whole population of the territory, the 'war' was waged, in defense of the American principle of the right of local self-government, of community self-preservation, though the resistance to the federal manifestation of force may not have been described at the time by such political terms."[1]

Stripped of its pro-Mormon overtones, the above statement would still remain a fairly accurate summation of the clash between Utah Mormons and their government.

By 1854, the expiration of Brigham Young's first term as governor of Utah Territory, events were stridently at work shaping the destiny of things so soon to follow. A year previous, Captain John W. Gunnison, heading a topographical survey of one of the proposed routes for the "Central Pacific Railroad" to California, was murdered, along with most of his small military escort. Unfortunately the "Gunnison massacre," at the hands of Pah-Utes, occurred in vicinity of the Mormon town of Fillmore. Though Mormons were completely exonerated of any complicity in the tragedy,[2] and the Indians responsible were brought to trial and sentence, the incident was avidly seized upon by Mormon-baiters in the east.

Kane's predicted clash between territorial office-appointees out of Washington and the Mormon people was a fact almost from the beginning. The meager salaries paid territorial officers ($1800 per annum for chief justice or secretary of the territory[3]), the isolated and undesirable nature of a sojourn in Utah, and the very evils inherent in the spoils system then running rampant, was hardly a guarantee that high-calibered and qualified officers would administer federal affairs in Zion.

[1]Roberts, *Comprehensive History*, vol. IV, p. 181.

[2]*Ibid.*, pp. 44-47.

[3]*Organic Act of Utah*, sec. ii.

"Among these 'foreign' appointees," says Roberts, "were adventurers who sought these appointments, not so much to serve the people among whom they were sent; nor to uphold the dignity, and national authority that appointed them; but to make their appointment a stepping stone to some personal advantage, political or otherwise. Others came for mere love of novelty and adventure. Others still in the hope that change of climate would arrest the progress of failing health, if not restore it; others being worn out, political hacks in their own community, accepted the appointment as the last reward for political party service. Others came with the idea there was a mission attachment to their office by which they were authorized and expected to engage in a crusade against the religion and the Church of the Latter-day Saints. All this, however, is said under recognition of the fact that there were honorable exceptions to this classification of the Utah 'foreign' appointee, though it must be said in candor, that the exceptions were rare."[4]

JUDGE BROCCHUS

One of the first of the "foreign" appointees to thoroughly entangle himself in the long hair of the Saints was the Hon. Perry E. Brocchus, associate justice for Utah Territory, and a political appointee of the Fillmore administration. The Brocchus head-on collision with the Mormon monolith was to become a factor contributing toward the major incident of the Utah War.

Brocchus had definite political ideas when he went west. At Kanesville (Council Bluffs), on his westward travels, he was reputed to have voiced hopes of being elected Utah's territorial representative. On his arrival in

[4]Roberts, *Comprehensive History,* vol. III, pp. 515-516.

BRIGHAM YOUNG VISITS UTAH'S COLONIES

—From Stenhouse's *Rocky Mountain Saints.*

Salt Lake City early in September of 1851 he unredeemably fumbled any chances of gaining the coveted post. In the delegation with Brocchus, seeing Utah for the first time, were appointees L. G. Brandebury, chief justice of United States court for Utah; B. D. Harris, secretary for Utah Territory, to serve under Governor Brigham Young; and H. R. Day, sub-Indian agent.

Before leaving for the west they had obligated themselves to arrange for a Utah contribution to the Washington Monument, then in process of erection—a block of native marble, which would join with other similar state and territorial offerings being molded into the towering edifice. However, their patriotic and moral senses, or at least that of Judge Brocchus, were offended by their first-hand introduction to the unabashed practice of Mormon "plural" marriage, along with the pulpit-zeal of Brigham Young and lesser leaders. The Mormon *Deseret News* had published *extenso* the July 24th ("Pioneer Day") oration of Daniel H. Wells, which took the government to task for its calm allowance of the past outrages against the Saints. In the same speech Wells castigated the administration for demanding the Mormon Battalion in the face of these injustices. Worse, he made uncomplimentary mention of Zachary Taylor, recently deceased.

Mormon conference was being held September 7, 8, and 9 in the "Bowery," and Brocchus requested of Governor Young the privilege of addressing the Saints. This curious request was granted. There are a number of written versions of what occurred. All seem to agree, generally, with Brigham Young's own report of the incident.

On the 7th, 8th and 9th I attended conference in the bowery. The Hon. Perry E. Brocchus, associate justice of the territory, requested the privilege of addressing the assembly. On being asked what would be his subject, he replied that he did not know. The privilege was granted, and on the second day of the conference he appeared in company with Judge Brandebury, Indian Superintendent Day, and several others of his friends, and addressed the congregation.

He expressed his everlasting gratitude for the kindness and hospitality of our people to him when sick and a stranger. He bore testimony to the peacefulness of the inhabitants of the territory, and their submission to the tribunals of their own choice, and prayed to God that all the United States might soon have such tribunals as were in this territory, and then it would always bring peace to the hearts of those who had to be judged. He hoped there would be no litigation. He denied that he came here with the view of being elected to congress, but had expressed his willingness to accept that office. if elected, and that he thought he could do us good in that way. He was an honorable man, or he would not have been appointed to office in this territory. He appeared before his audience, under a commission by the board of managers of the National Washington Monument, to ask the territory to contribute a block of marble towards the erection of that building. He cursorily reviewed the career and character of George Washington.

He then referred to the oration of Hon. D. H. Wells on the 24th of July, and objected to some portions of it. The government made no imperative demand for 500 of our best men for service in the Mexican War, and had no evil intentions in asking for them, nor was it responsible for the persecutions in Missouri and Illinois. President Polk expressed decided disapprobation of these deeds, he [Brocchus] felt indignant about them, and he believed the mass of people, at the time, boiled with rage towards the perpetrators. The federal government had not injured us. The president could not lay a private wrong before congress. To those states [i.e. Missouri and Illinois], we should look for redress.

The speaker regretted to hear in our midst such expressions as that the United States were a stink in our nostrils. He was pained to hear it said that the government of the United States was going to hell as fast as possible. He said that if the people of Utah could not offer a block [of marble] for the Washington Monument in full fellowship with the United States, it were better to leave it unquarried in the bosom of the native mountain. He directed a portion of his discourse towards the ladies, and, libertine as he boasted himself, *strongly recommended them to become virtuous.*

The Mormon audience had listened restlessly to the barbed speech, but when Brocchus singled out the ladies for his remarks on virtue, the place instantly became a clamorous uproar. Brigham Young instantly arose to defend his flock.

"Judge Brocchus is either profoundly ignorant or wilfully wicked, one or the two. There are several gentlemen on this platform who would be glad to prove the statements referred to in relation to him, and much more, if he would let them have the stand. His speech is designed to have political bearing. If I permit discussion to arise here, there may be either pulling of hair or a cutting of throats. It is well known to every man in this community, and has become a matter of history throughout the enlightened world, that the government of the United States looked on the scenes of robbing, driving, and murdering of this people and said nothing about the matter, but by silence gave sanction to the lawless proceedings. Hundreds of women and children have been laid in the tomb prematurely in consequence thereof, and their blood cries to the Father for vengeance against those who have caused or consented to their death. George Washington was not dandied in the cradle of ease, but schooled to a life of hardship in exploring and surveying the mountains and defending the frontier settlers, even in his early youth, from the tomahawk and the scalping knife. It was God that dictated him and enabled him to assert and maintain the independence of the country. It is the same God that leads this people. I love the government and the Constitution of the United States, but I do not love the damned rascals who administer the government.

"I know Zachary Taylor, he is dead and damned, and I cannot help it. I am indignant at such corrupt fellows as Judge Brocchus coming here to lecture us on morality and virtue. I could buy a thousand of such men and put them in a bandbox. Ladies and gentlemen, here we learn principle and good manners. It is an insult to this congregation to throw out such insinuations. I say it is an insult, and I will say no more."[5]

It was evident that Brocchus had stumbled disastrously in his path toward popularity with the Saints. An exchange of letters between himself and Young indicates that the judge had intended no militant attack upon either morals or beliefs of the Mormon people. But already the mistake was beyond repair.

The Washington-appointed Secretary of the Territory, B. D. Harris, further complicated matters by persistently feuding with Governor Young regarding the administration of the organic act previous to the new secretary's arrival. Specifically, Harris was dissatisfied in the manner the governor had taken "the enumeration of the inhabitants of the new territory," before the first election under the act, which census was to form the basis for apportioning the representatives and councilors of the various counties. He was unhappy about the conduct of the election, as the Mormons, apparently, had not executed it within the precise framework and within the niceties of procedure which the secretary had blueprinted for his portfolio. And all of it had been conducted "without the seal of the territory or signature of the secretary."[6]

In his capacity as governor of the territory, Brigham Young was far more conciliatory and cooperative than in his role as head of the church. He answered Harris by citing the fact "that nearly a year had elapsed since the appointment of the territorial officers, during which time the people of Utah, nevertheless, were living without authorized government," and that his people had gone

[5] *History of Brigham Young, Ms.*, entry for Sept. 8, 1851, pp. 61-64. Quoted in Roberts, *Comprehensive History*, vol. III, pp. 522-523.

[6] "Utah Officials" Report, *Congressional Globe*, vol. xxv, p. 8, new series.

ahead with census and elections according to the best light possible under the conditions. "This being previous to the arrival of the secretary," he explained, "of course his seal and signature was not attached."[7]

UTAH'S "RUN-AWAY OFFICIALS"

But already Harris and Brocchus, together with the other appointees, had concluded the Mormon Zion was not for them. They gave notice of their intent to return east, and of taking with them the federal funds apportioned to the territory, along with the territorial seal.

Governor Young acted by immediately calling a session of the legislature, to which Harris disdainfully refused to attend, or act in function of his office. "Two days later the legislature passed a joint resolution authorizing ths United States marshal to take into his custody all papers, records, documents and property of every kind pertaining to said office of secretary, as also all money in his possession belonging to said territory, and safely keep the same until the legislature should order otherwise. This resolution was presented to Mr. Harris together with an order for five hundred dollars to defray the incidental expenses of the legislative assembly."[8]

Harris refused to comply to either of these demands. Brandebury and Brocchus assembled the Supreme Court, which judicial panel promptly handed down an injunction "forbidding the marshal and others from seizing or intermeddling with the funds and other property of the United States in the custody of the secretary."[9] Harris was successful in keeping both seal and money out of Mormon hands.

[7]Roberts, *Comprehensive History*, vol. III, p. 530.

[8]*Ibid.*, vol. III, p. 532.

[9]Documents in the case are quoted *extenso* in *Congressional Globe*, vol. xxv, new series, pp. 88 01.

On September 28 he, together with Brandebury, Brocchus and Day, shook the dust of Zion off their heels and headed east. At St. Louis the "run-away officials" deposited the articles and money in their possession with the assistants federal treasurer at that point. In Washington they made full report of the affair to President Millard Fillmore, together with charges against Governor Young. Complaints against Utah's territorial governor ran the scale from misconduct of office to embezzlement and immorality.

The effect was like a bombshell. And as the newspapers played upon the theme, every point of the controversy was aired and argued. In time the hysterical outcry against Brigham Young and his Mormons crystallized into two general patterns of thought; (a) Why was Brigham Young, in the face of all such alleged malfeasance and wrong-doing allowed to act as governor of the territory?; (b) general disgust for the cowardice of the officers who had fled their posts.[10]

The "run-away officials," in spite of the public outcry generated by their dramatic flight from Zion, failed to provoke either President Fillmore or Congress to any official move against Brigham Young or the Saints. Their report and charges made sensational newspaper copy across the land, but were nullified as instruments for governmental action by the public clamor raised by their inglorious exit in the face of danger. Added to this was the editorial amusement occasioned by asinine platform blowings by Brocchus, even after his return, and the mirth provoked by his written charges.[11] The public was being treated to a peculiar phenomenon, in that the whirlwind so successfully generated in far-away Utah had by now caught up with and was unmercifully whipping the ones who had started the forces a-spin.

In the *New York Herald* there appeared the first of a series of letters humorously castigating the "run-away officials" and biting back at the ridicule and criticism being heaped upon Governor Young and the Mormons generally. The letters were over the signature of Jedediah M. Grant, first mayor of Salt Lake City—at the time serv-

[10]"But these judges—at least one of them, Judge Brocchus, seems to have considered that new duties were added to his judicial functions. In the states, and well regulated communities, it is considered to be decorous, and the duty of the judges, to keep entirely free from popular excitement—that they may stand forth as the arbiters between the community and the government, and between man and man. Judge Brocchus it seems, summoned the people to assemble: they listened to him respectfully: whilst he made a speech against them and their criminal practices. This may be the province of a territorial judge, but we are at a loss for the statute requiring it. It could hardly be expected, that a fanatical and misled people—such as we all believe the Mormons to be—would not be roused to anger, and indeed to make violent demonstrations, by such an assault upon them and their leaders. . . We think the judges should have remained at their posts, proceeded regularly with their courts, kept out of excitement, and when cases occurred requiring the exercise of their official authority, exercised it fearlessly and without favor or affection. If they had done this, and their authority had been resisted, then, and not until then, the public would have been prepared to excuse their retreat.

"For Mr. Harris, there is quite as little excuse. So far as the published statements go, he does not seem to have been seriously interfered with in anything except the effort to take money which he had the legal custody of. In all his other acts he had no opposition, and in this case, when the court decided in his favor, the governor and his people submitted.

"But, what surpasses our comprehension is, what a subagent of the Utah Indians has to do with the civil and political affairs of the people of the Utah territory, unless they conflict in some way with the Indians. Yet Mr. Day also finds an apology in this seditious language, to leave the Indians to the mercies of these corrupt and seditious people and come back to the states. One would have supposed that he could have discharged his duties to the Indians at least, even if Governor Young had committed treason, and been hanged for it."

—*St. Louis Republican*, Nov. 25, 1851. Reprinted also in *Deseret News*, Feb. 7, 1852.

[11]Stenhouse, Tullidge and nearly every writer on this subject quotes the now-famous passage from one of the alleged reports sent to Washington by these harassed officials, that "polygamy monopolized all the women, which made it very inconvenient for the federal officers to live here" {in Utah} . It is impossible to find the document or letter from which this statement is allegedly taken.

ing in missionary capacity in the eastern states. Strangely, Grant was not the author of these attempts at Mormon rebuttal. Stenhouse mentions how "painful" it was to him to learn that "two of Pennsylvania's honored sons . . . one no less than an ex-vice-president of the United States, and the other enjoying a military title—were the inspiration and authors of the famous letters."[12] Colonel Thomas L. Kane was one of the "honored sons" responsible for the Grant-signed letters. The letters' content, while satirical and amusing in themselves, fell far short of explaining away the charges the "run-away officials" had blasted Zionward. President Fillmore, final target of public clamor, had already considered the necessity of removing Brigham Young as territorial governor.

The charges against Young—immorality, malfeasance and treason—were as embarrassing as they were serious, and politicians of every quarter and party were making capital of them. With a sense of fairness and a hunger for truth remarkable in a day of political hatcheting, Millard Fillmore turned, in his perplexity, to Thomas L. Kane. Fillmore in his note, reminded Kane that as president he had relied much upon him "for the moral character and standing of Mr. Young." "You knew him," said the president, and "I doubt not will truly state whether these charges against him are true."

[12]Stenhouse, T. B. H., *Rocky Mountain Saints,* p. 278. The authors were undoubtedly Col. Thomas L. Kane and ex-Vice-President George M. Dallas.

"President Young remarks upon these letters: 'Elder Jedediah M. Grant wrote me from New York, May 13th, that he had ready for circulation his letters to the *New York Herald* in pamphlet form, a copy of which he was about to send to each member of congress and to the principal editors of the nation. His letters contained a refutation of the charges made by the returned federal officers against myself and the inhabitants of Utah, and were written in a humorous, readable style; *for which they were principally indebted to the versatile pen of our friend Colonel Thomas L. Kane."—History of Brigham Young, Ms.,* entry, June 1852, p. 56. See also Roberts, *Comprehensive History,* III, p. 528.

Philadelphia, July , 1851.

My Dear Sir:—I have no wish to evade the responsibility of having vouched for the character of Mr. Brigham Young, of Utah, and his fitness for the station he now occupies. I reiterate without reserve, the statement of his excellent capacity. energy, and integrity. which I made prior to his appointment. I am willing to say I volunteered to communicate to you facts by which I was convinced of his patriotism, and devotion to the interests of the Union. I made no qualification when I assured you of his irreproachable moral character, because I was able to speak of this from my own intimate personal knowledge.

If any show or shadow of evidence can be adduced in support of the charges of your anonymous assailant, the next mail from Utah shall bring you their complete and circumstantial refutation. Meanwhile I am ready to offer this assurance for publication in any form you care to indicate, and challenge contradiction from any respectable authority.

I am, Sir, with high respect and esteem, your most obedient servant,

[Signed] THOMAS L. KANE.[13]

In his correspondence with Millard Fillmore, and the Grant-signed letters to the *New York Herald.* Kane had put the Mormon people more securely in his debt. There is no question that Kane's vigorous defense, coming as it did from an impeccable Gentile source, weighed heavily for Utah's favor in Washington. In spite of Brocchus, Harris, and their fugitive retinue, Brigham Young remained in his post as governor of Utah Territory. And the new panel of appointees found Zion tolerable enough to remain in tenure. But in vouching for Brigham Young's "irreproachable moral character" Kane had acted with more zeal than knowledge.

Polygamous marriages had been an accepted thing, at least among the leaders, long before the Saints had set foot in Great Salt Lake Valley. In 1843, two years before

[13]For letter and previous quotation see Roberts, III, p. 538.

his murder at Carthage, Illinois, Joseph Smith, as prophet, had received his heavenly revelation setting forth in detail the pattern of "celestial marriage." Kane, in his visit to the Mormons in 1846, apparently had not been let in on the secret—for by that time Brigham had added several wives to his famous "increase," and most of the Mormon dignitaries around him had been diligently pursuing the doctrine.

By the time Judge Brocchus publicly invited the Mormon women to step out of the pattern and "become virtuous," the practice was well enough established in Utah to have become common knowledge. Officially the Church had evaded any public mention of the highly interesting situation which had developed within its ranks. Even while Kane was reassuring a worried President Fillmore regarding Brigham's moral rectitude, many a Gentile wayfarer had verified what practically every Mormon in Utah knew to be a fact. And yet, so long as the Church remained non-committal on the score, the burden of proof between fact and rumor still lay upon the Gentiles. On August 28, 1852 rumor and truth dramatically joined hands.

On that date, at a general conference of the Church, held in Salt Lake City, Apostle Orson Pratt blew the lid off the Mormon steam-kettle by announcing to the world that "plural marriages" not only existed, but were part and parcel of the Church's theology and creed. In the afternoon session Brigham Young verified what Elder Pratt had stated, elaborated on the doctrine from the standpoint of spiritual salvation, and backed its authenticity from the Prophet's own revelation.

What formerly were only rumblings of thunder became an explosion that was heard around the world—the reverberations of which, to this day, have never died out.

Mormons at last had given flesh into which their enemies could sink teeth. Yet, in spite of the tumult, the friendship of Thomas L. Kane never wavered. Henceforth, however, it would take much more than any word from Kane to guide Washington's policy in Mormon behalf. The match had been touched to Utah's powder-keg.

LIEUT.-GENERAL BRIGHAM YOUNG,
NAUVOO LEGION

—From *Contributor,* Vol. IX.

V

Steptoe Steps In

WITH the political dumping of Millard Fillmore, and election of Franklin Pierce as fourteenth President of the United States, more cognizance was taken of the public clamor against Governor Brigham Young and his Saints. Mormon announcement of the doctrine and practice of "plural marriage" close on the heels of the Brocchus-Brandebury-Harris-Day accusations congealed American opinion. Brigham Young would not be reappointed at the close of his term of office, 1854.

"I deeply regret to inform you," wrote Utah's delegate Bernhisel to Apostle Franklin D. Richards, "that the president [Pierce] finally declined to reappoint Governor Young to the office he now holds." The new appointee was Colonel E. J. Steptoe. And Steptoe's Utah-bound retinue would include a small army of United States soldiers. "The colonel," Bernhisel hopefully adds, "sustains a high character here [in Washington], and numbers among his friends the honorable secretary of war [Jefferson Davis]. Since Governor Young's reappointment could not be secured, which is a source of profound regret to us all, I know of no one who, I suppose, would be more acceptable than Colonel Steptoe, but his friends here believe he will not accept."[1]

Brigham himself did not precisely concur with Bernhisel in regard to Steptoe being acceptable. "We have got a territorial government, and I am and will be the governor," he trumpeted from the pulpit, "and no power can hinder it until the Lord Almighty says, 'Brigham, you need not be governor any longer,' and then I am willing to yield to another."[2] Though Brigham, in his sermon, was talking of God's prerogative to lift him from office, the American press interpreted the remarks as pointing defiance at President Pierce. Another storm rolled out from Zion.

Colonel Edward J. Steptoe, with two companies of artillery, and one company of infantry, arrived in Salt Lake City on August 31, 1854. With him were 150 wagon-men and quartermaster's-men, 100 wagons, and 1,000 head of horses and mules. All in all, it was an impressive array of power. In addition to carrying credentials as governor of the territory, Steptoe had been given orders to arrest and bring to trial the perpetrators of the Gunnison massacre. Apparently satisfied that Indians, rather than Mormons, were concerned with the atrocity, he and a portion of his command took only a sharp-eyed spectators' part in the trial and conviction of the Indians responsible for the affair.

Apparently Steptoe too was satisfied that all was well in Zion, or at least Brigham Young would do better at governing the peculiar Mormons than a Gentile military man. He delayed, and finally refrained entirely from presenting his credentials as governor. Moreover he, and the

[1]*Millennial Star*, vol. XVII, p. 110. Letter dated Jan. 4, 1854.

officers of his command, joined with all the federal appointees to office and the Gentile merchants of Salt Lake City in petitioning President Pierce to reinstate Brigham Young as the territorial head.[3] This course Franklin Pierce followed — to the amazement and dismay of Congress and the eastern press.

Aside from the furor occasioned by Pierce's failure to replace Young, considerable speculation immediately arose as to why Steptoe refused to take over the territorial government. Fifteen years later Vice-President Schuyler Colfax, elected with U. S. Grant in 1868, asserted that "Colonel Steptoe was commissioned as governor, in the place of Young; but after wintering with a battalion of soldiers at Salt Lake, he resigned, not deeming it safe or prudent to accept."[4] Mrs. C. B. Waite draws a touching picture of the gallant colonel being seduced by a pair of beautiful Mormon women acting under the direction of Brigham Young. In order to escape exposure for his indiscreet and compromising act, the colonel was assertedly forced to resign as governor, and recommend Brigham Young in his place."[5]

[2]Sermon quoted in *Deseret News*, March 16, 1854. See *Journal of Discourses*, I, pp. 187-188.

[3]The petition, with all signatures attached, was published in *Deseret News*, Sept. 2, 1857.

[4]See Colfax's communication to the *New York Independent*, Dec. 2, 1869.

[5]Waite, Mrs. C. B., *The Mormon Prophet*, 1866. Mrs. Waite was wife of Judge Charles B. Waite, an associate justice to Utah under Lincoln's appointment. Mrs. Waite states in her book that the narrative of Steptoe's downfall was "furnished by a Mormon who was residing in Utah at the time" (p. 27). Bancroft states "There are no grounds for such a statement." (*History of Utah*, p. 493, note.) However, Linn, Beadle, and others have used and embellished the story in their writings.

Actually, in his 1854-55 wintering in Utah, Colonel Steptoe seems to have gotten along very well with the Mormon people. His reluctance to present credentials as governor left the territory with a vacancy to the office, until the subsequent reappointment of Brigham Young to his former position.

The Saints, however, remained outspoken in their criticism of the Pierce administration and its seeming willingness to bow to the anti-Mormon clamor throughout the states; yet little, if any, criticism was leveled at Steptoe personally. "But I will say, to the praise of the gallant gentleman referred to [Steptoe]," said Brigham, "if there was going to be a gentleman called upon to be our governor, there is not a man, out of the kingdom of God [meaning the Latter-day Saint Church], that I would listen to sooner, and feel more confidence and cordiality towards, than him. I wish this need of praise could be awarded every officer in the government, but it cannot."[6]

In comment of Steptoe's expected appointment, Apostle Orson Hyde wrote the *Deseret News:* "So far as I am acquainted, there is no man in the territory, outside the church, who shares, more liberally, the respect and confidence of her citizens than the colonel . . ." And then, in gentle nudge at the colonel: "Colonel S. is not obliged to accept his appointment; and it remains to be seen whether he entertains a similar respect for *popular sovereignty* and the known wishes of the great mass of the citizens of the territory to that which they entertain for him."[7] Steptoe's accedance to "popular sovereignty" settled the issue of governorship with peaceful finality. To the east only went the anguished howls of Congress and the American press.

William Hickman, in his startling memoirs, disposes of the Steptoe affair in a single paragraph: "In the fall of

1854, Col. E. J. Steptoe came to Salt Lake City with three hundred United States troops, and wintered in the city. They got along peaceably until Christmas Day, when a portion of them and a good many citizens got drunk. They had a regular street fight, and there were a good many sore heads and bloody noses on both sides. But the officers put a stop to this, and all was quiet the next day. I got in town just in time to see the crowd dispersing. In the spring, Col. Steptoe went to California with his troops . . ."[8]

Had Steptoe, instead of continuing on to California, elected to remain on as Utah's governor, the turbulent history of the next three years might have been favorably altered. While he had satisfied himself as to the tranquility and peace of the Mormon Zion, and had convinced President Pierce of the Saints' ability to conduct and control their own public affairs, still many grave problems remained unresolved. The sources of friction continued on as before. The anti-Mormon critics had been given no appeasement. The veil of mistrust and misunderstanding was even more tightly drawn across the promised land.

[8]Hickman, William, *Brigham's Destroying Angel*, p. 107.

VI

The World of the Saints

A MAJOR task confronting the Mormons on their arrival in Salt Lake Valley was the setting up of a workable form of civil government, with police, courts, and magistrates. The pioneering epics of Oregon, California and other areas of the west have little in common with the great Mormon experiment in Utah. First of all, this movement was strictly religious in character. The entire colony was unified in a single faith. There was little diversity of thought. Latter-day Saints honestly believed they were building the "Kingdom of God"[1] on earth.

It must also be considered that they had sought out their promised land as a haven from oppression, with the one obsessive thought of colonizing far from their former angry and hostile neighbors. Any move, therefore, which threatened the peace of their existence or the tranquility of their vision, no matter from what source, was con-

[1]This thought has never ceased to prevail among the Latter-day Saints, and is still an essential part of Mormon theology. The Church considers itself the original, restored gospel of Jesus Christ; the one and only door for the redemption and salvation of mankind.

sidered in the light of harassment and persecution. So, if the judiciary and legislative functions of Zion smacked closely of Mormon theocracy and bishops' courts, there was reason for it. Religion was center focus and motivation for Mormon existence in those first hard years of winning a foothold in an hostile, forbidding land.

Governmental appointees sent out of Washington to manage territorial affairs faced a problem necessitating tact and diplomacy without parallel. To Mormons they were "Gentiles,"[2] with motives open to suspicion, and whose views could never coincide with the initiated. Nor did the appointees themselves always contribute toward an understanding between Saints and those whom the Saints considered their persecutors. Too often the appointees were merely political hacks and hangers-on, tendered minor territorial posts as election rewards, or banished scapegoats sent out to the frontiers as punishment for political traducement.

Up to the explosive year of 1857 the friction and conflict between Gentile officeholders and the Mormon theocracy had been constant and bitter. As natural consequence, those appointees who were sent to Utah, and who could neither work with nor condone Mormon ideology, flooded the receptive east with long and bitter complaints. It was difficult to understand, let alone abide, the smug and unbending attitude of those whom they were sent to govern, and toward whom they were expected to administer and dispense justice.

MORMON COURTS

An abrasive annoyance to the federal jurists, which eventually grew to calamitous proportions, was the territory's system of probate courts. These were simply

[2] To a Latter-day Saint even a Jew is a Gentile, unless an adherent to the faith.

outgrowths of the earlier Mormon bishops' courts, wherein neighbors gathered to hear and arbitrate their grievances under the friendly counsel of some respected member of their ward[3]—usually the ward bishop. Seldom were any of these men trained jurists. All of them were members of the Mormon priesthood.[4] But no one could deny that verdicts handed down by these rustic tribunals were remarkable for their sense of justice, impartiality, and honest adherence to the letter of truth.

Probate and district courts were authorized by the territorial legislature of 1851-1852—the first session held under the Organic Act. District courts were saddled with the proviso that "by the consent of the court and the parties, any person may be selected to act as judge for the trial of any particular cause or question; and while thus acting he shall possess all the powers of the district judge in the case." Simplicity was to be the keynote, for "with a view to the attainment of justice . . . all technical forms of action and pleadings, are hereby abolished."

Of the probate courts there was provided one judge in each county, elected by the legislature, but commissioned by the governor. In addition to the mundane duties of probating wills and administration of estate and guardianship matters the probate courts were granted the heavier responsibilities of "original jurisdiction, both civil and criminal, and as well in chancery as at common law." Prosecuting attorneys, appointed by the probate court judges, were charged "to attend to all legal business in the county, in which the territory is a party, and prose-

[3]A Mormon "ward" was not only an ecclesiastical division of a community similar to a parish, but a geographical one as well.

[4]All male members of the Latter-day Saints Church, from twelve years of age upward, are members of its priesthood. There are two divisions of Mormon priesthood: the lower, or Aaronic; the higher, or Melchizedek.

SOUTH TEMPLE STREET, SALT LAKE CITY — "THE PROPHET'S BLOCK"

—From Burton's *City of the Saints*

cute before the probate court of his county, all individuals accused of crimes."[5]

Nearly every office, from attorney-general to county marshals, clerks, and deputies, were appointive from the legislature, and amenable to it. To the federal officers sent out from Washington, this constituted the great Mormon freeze-out. By design or accident, it managed to keep Mormon affairs very much in Mormon hands.

It was not uncommon for one man in a community to hold a multiple of public offices, and still serve as Ward Bishop or Stake President in ecclesiastical affairs.[6]

THE JUDICIAL FERMENT

Many were the clashes between Gentile judges and the oddly constituted courts. John F. Kinney, territorial chief justice; William W. Drummond of Illinois, and George P. Stiles, an ex-Mormon (excommunicated for adultery)—all three appointees of President Pierce—were the trio which finally brought the judicial turbulence into eruption.

By February of 1857 a noisy argument as to whether it was the federal or territorial right to serve writs or impanel juries reached a climax in the court of Judge Stiles. The judge, regarded by the Saints as fallen from the

[5]Enactment approved Feb. 4, 1852. *Laws of Utah*, 1852.

[6]"When I first went to Salt Lake City, the Robt. T. Burton often mentioned by Hickman, was Collector of Internal Revenue for the Territory, Sheriff of the County, Assessor and Collector of Territorial Taxes, besides being Bishop of the Church, General in the Nauvoo Legion, and husband of four wives . . . One man in Fillmore held the offices of County Clerk and Recorder; Town Clerk and Justice of the Peace; Assessor and Collector of Internal Revenue, and *ex-officio* Overseer of the Poor."—Beadle appendix, Hickman, *Brigham's Destroying Angel*, p. 205.

priesthood and unworthy of respect,[7] had issued certain writs to the United States Marshal which some of the legalistic Saints felt were more properly under local jurisdiction. A brace of Mormon attorneys, led by James Ferguson, and including Hosea Stout and J. C. Little, abruptly entered Stiles' courtroom, and by boisterous conduct and threats proceeded to break up court and intimidate the judge.

In high anger, Stiles adjourned his court, and appealed to Governor Brigham Young. Next the Mormon hotheads raided Stiles' law office, seized his books and papers, and burned them in the judge's privy.

Brigham Young's viewance of the disturbance, and his answer to Stiles' appeal, did little to steady the hand of federal jurisprudence in Utah. "If you cannot sustain and enforce the laws," Brigham reportedly told the judge, "the sooner you adjourn your court the better."[8]

JUDGE DRUMMOND

The handling of Judge William W. Drummond was even less delicate. Tact, apparently, was no part of Drummond's makeup. One of his first acts upon arrival in Utah was to brusquely and publicly announce his intention to ignore all special powers given to probate courts by territorial enactment. He denounced the courts as

[7]"Stiles had been more or less prominent in 'Mormon' affairs from Nauvoo times. In Nauvoo he held the office of city attorney and in the city council advocated the destruction of the *Nauvoo Expositor*. He had latterly, however, fallen into evil ways, and had been excommunicated from the church in the preceding December, by the conjoint action of a number of the apostles and a general meeting of the seventies—of which latter body the judge was a member—for immoral conduct—adultery. This loss of moral standing in the community, doubtless contributed to a lack of respect for his court . . ." — Roberts, *Comprehensive History*, vol. IV, p. 199.

[8]See Bancroft's *History of Utah*, p. 489. Also Waite's *Mormon Prophet*, pp. 36-37; Linn's *Story of the Mormons*, pp. 470-471.

having been "founded in ignorance," and their decisions as having no binding effect.

It was not legal interpretations or decisions, however, which fouled Drummond's nest in Zion. "Judge Drummond's course in Utah was in many ways scandalous," writes Linn, who could scarcely be called a Mormon-lover.[9] A "gambler and bully," was Bancroft's appraisal of Drummond.[10] But that was high praise compared to the Mormon verdict. News trailing his western safari was to the effect he had deserted a wife and family back in Oquawka, Illinois.[11] The mistress he brought west with him irked and nettled the puritanistic Saints, who stressed the necessity and sanctity of marriage, and considered it an insult when a female of an adulterous relationship was allowed to share bench with the judge while he handed down his pompous and unpopular decrees.

Public criticism of the Gentile judge quickly rose to fury. Mormon newspapers began commenting on Drummond's loose living, gambling and drunkenness. The judge lashed back at Mormon stiff-neckedness and polygamy. Levi Abrahams, a Mormon-converted Jewish shopkeeper in Fillmore, made a too-personal remark—so personal that Judge Drummond dispatched Cato, his Negro body servant, to horsewhip the Jew. Cato did a thorough job of it.

Mormons retaliated by arresting both the judge and his servant.

[9]Linn, William A., *Story of the Mormons*, p. 469.

[10]Bancroft, Hubert Howe, *History of Utah*, p. 490.

[11]Mrs. Drummond's letter, confirming this, was published in *Deseret News*, May 20, 1857. See also Remy, Jules, *Journey to Great Salt Lake*, vol. I, pp. 208-209.

Drummond, with the help of Justice John F. Kinney, succeeded in "smothering" the case—but not the hatred and clamor which followed. It was amid howl and fury that Judge William W. Drummond made a final fast exit from Utah Territory.

In California, before taking ship for the "states," Judge Drummond raised a vicious outcry against the Mormons and their treatment of him. The San Francisco press, acting as mouthpiece to the judge's vituperations, joined with him in denouncing the sect.[12] On his arrival in New Orleans Judge Drummond mailed his resignation to United States Attorney-General Jeremiah Black, including with it enough accusations against Brigham Young to hang him. The explosive document included the following points:

1. That Brigham Young is head of the "Mormon" church; and, as such head, the "Mormons" look to him alone, for the law by which they are to be governed; therefore no law of congress is by them considered binding in any matter.

2. That he (Drummond) knew that a secret, oathbound organization existed among all the male members of the church to resist the laws of the country, and to acknowledge no law save the law of the priesthood, which came to the people through Brigham Young.

3. That there were a number of men "set apart by special order of the church, to take both the lives and property of any person who may question the authority of the church."

"That the records, papers, etc., of the supreme court have been destroyed by order of the church, with the direct knowledge and approbation of Governor B. Young, and the federal

[12]See the *San Francisco Bulletin, Alta California,* and the *Sacramento Daily Union, passim.* Mormon refutation of the judge's attack was published in *Western Standard,* San Francisco.

officers grossly insulted for presuming to raise a single question about the treasonable act."[13]

4. That the federal officers of the territory are constantly insulted, harassed, and annoyed by the Mormons, and for these insults there is no redress.

5. That the federal officers are daily compelled to hear the form of the American government traduced, the chief executives of the nation, both living and dead, slandered and abused from the masses as well as from all the leading members of the church.

6. The judge charged discrimination in the administration of the laws as against Mormon and Gentile; that Captain John W. Gunnison and his party were murdered by Indians but "under the orders, advice and direction of the Mormons;" that the Mormons poisoned Judge Leonidas Shaver, Drummond's predecessor; that Almon W. Babbitt, secretary of the territory, had been killed on the plains by a band of Mormons, instead of by Indians as reported from Utah.[14]

In the document Judge Drummond emphatically contended that troops were necessary to enforce any laws made and presented by the government at Washington, or by any of its appointees in the Territory of Utah.

Seriousness of Drummond's charges did not go unheeded by Washington, the politicians, the nation's pulpit, nor the press. No one could doubt the judge had truly and fearfully exploded a bomb over the heads of the Mormon people.

Curtis E. Bolton, deputy clerk of Utah's Supreme Court, made immediate and sworn denial to

[13]"Such excuse as existed for making this report arose from the fact that at the time of the disturbance in Judge Stiles' court, a number of books and papers were taken from the judge's office during his absence and burned. As the records, papers, etc., of the supreme court of the territory were supposed to be kept in his office it was suspected that they were also destroyed, whereas they were safe in the custody of the deputy clerk of the supreme court, Curtis E. Bolton . . ." — Roberts, *Comprehensive History*, vol. V, p. 203, note.

[14]The Resignation, in *extenso* will be found in *House Executive Documents*, 35th Congress, 1st session, X, No. 71, p. 212.

Drummond's charges of judicial sabotage. "The records, papers, etc. of the supreme court in this territory, together with all decisions and documents of every kind belonging thereto . . . are all safe and complete in my custody, and not one of them missing, nor have they been disturbed by any person."[15]

Drummond's accusations reaped pointed denial from other quarters as well. On April 15 a statement from Feramorz Little, of the Western Mail Service, was sent to the *New York Herald* and was published April 25 in summary and abbreviated form. "The charges of Judge Drummond are as false as he is corrupt. Before I left for the States, I was five days every week in Great Salt Lake City, and I witness to all the world that I never heard one word of the burning of nine hundred volumes of law records, etc., nor anything of that character . . . The treasonable acts alleged against the Mormons in Utah are false from beginning to end . . ."

For the most part, however, there was little editorial sympathy rendered the Mormon side of the controversy. Judge Drummond's blast was generally accepted as credible expose of a seditious people in open rebellion against the government of the United States.

Another uproar had to do with the mails, which, up to now had been carried west to Utah by the firm of Hockaday & Magraw, at a contract price of $50,000 per year. In that same chaotic year of 1857, at the opening of governmental mail bids, the canny Brigham Young, and his "B.Y. Express and Carrying Company" (Y.X. Company), submitted a devastatingly low bid of $23,600 per year, and the government's mail passed immediately into

[15]*House Executive Documents*, 35th Congress, 1st session, X, No. 71, pp. 214-215. Published also in the *St. Louis Republican*, issue of July 26, 1857.

Mormon hands. W. M. F. Magraw was no man to take defeat lightly.

From Independence, Missouri, Magraw wrote a stinging letter to the new president, James Buchanan: "No vestige of law and order [in Utah], no protection of life or property; the civil laws of the territory are overshadowed and neutralized by a so-styled ecclesiastical organization, as despotic, dangerous, and damnable, as has ever been known to exist in any country . . ."[16]

In President Buchanan, Magraw and Drummond found ready ear. It needed only Almon W. Babbitt's tragic death (appointive secretary of Utah Territory) on the plains to give rallying point to public sentiment against the Saints. Babbitt, with a small entourage, had been on his way to Utah to take up office. After leaving Fort Leavenworth toward the west, the party was never again seen alive by white men. Later the discovery of Babbitt's watch on the person of a Cheyenne Indian brought confession from a number of the tribesmen that they had perpetrated the massacre in retaliation for soldier outrages suffered by their people.[17] In the general uproar Mormons were immediately accused of the deed.

[16]Magraw's Letter to the President. *House Executive Documents*, 35th Congress, 1st session, X, No. 71, pp. 2-3.

[17]See Julia Ann Babbitt's statement, *Crescent City Oracle*, copied into *Millennial Star*, vol. XIX, p. 443.

COLONEL A. W. BABBITT'S MURDER

Interesting letter from his widow – Her melancholy investigation of the circumstances of His Death – The Cheyenne Indians His Assassins . . .

"I have not a shadow of suspicion that white men were in any way concerned in his death—the newspaper story that he was killed by the 'Mormons' to the contrary notwithstanding. As an act of public justice I ask you to lay these facts before the people, that my friends and the many friends of my husband may know the facts relative to his melancholy death." Signed "JULIA ANN BABBITT." — Statement and letter copied from *New York Herald*, Roberts, *Comp. Hist.*, vol. IV, pp. 213-214.

Violent as were the charges, President Buchanan and his administration were far ahead of public sentiment. In spite of the fact that no official investigation had yet been made as to whether accusations were true or false, the "Utah Expedition" was secretly projected and organized. Within sixty days its first army supply trains were moving out of Fort Leavenworth toward Salt Lake City.

VII

The Utah Expedition

SENATOR STEPHEN A. DOUGLAS, "strong man" of the administration, apparently assumed the task of carrying the government's anti-Mormon program to the people. While troops assembled at Fort Leavenworth, Douglas went vocally and politically to work on the subject. The most famous of his "Mormon" orations was delivered at Springfield, Illinois. June 12, 1857—five weeks before the vanguard of the Utah Expedition started its march westward:

> If we are permitted to place credence in the rumors and reports from that country (and it must be admitted that they have increased and strengthened and assumed consistency and plausibility by each succeeding mail), seven years' experience has disclosed a state of facts entirely different from that which was supposed to exist when Utah was organized. These rumors and reports would seem to justify the belief that the following tracts are susceptible of proof.
>
> *1st.* That nine-tenths of the inhabitants are aliens by birth, who have refused to become naturalized, or to take the oath of

allegiance, or to do any other act recognizing the government of the United States as the paramount authority in that territory.

2nd. That all the inhabitants, whether native or alien born, known as Mormons (and they constitute the whole people of the territory), are bound by horrid oaths and terrible penalties, to recognize and maintain the authority of Brigham Young, and the government of which he is the head, as paramount to that of the United States, in civil as well as religious affairs; and they will, in due time, and under the direction of their leaders, use all the means in their power to subvert the government of the United States, and resist its authority.

3rd. That the Mormon Government, with Brigham Young at its head, is now forming alliance with Indian tribes in Utah and adjoining territories—stimulating the Indians to acts of hostility—organizing bands of his own followers under the name of "Danites" or "Destroying Angels," to prosecute a system of robbery and murders upon American citizens, who support the authority of the United States, and denounce the infamous and disgusting practices and institutions of the Mormon government.

. . . Let us have these facts in official shape before the president and congress, and the country will soon learn that, in the performance of the high and solemn duty devolving upon the executive and congress, there will be no vacillating or hesitating policy. It will be as prompt as the peal that follows the flash—as stern and unyielding as death. Should such a state of things actually exist as we are led to infer from the reports—and such information comes in an official shape—the knife must be applied to this pestiferous, disgusting cancer, which is gnawing into the very vitals of the body politic. It must be cut out by the roots, and seared over by the red hot iron of stern and unflinching law . . .[1]

The vituperation of Senator Douglas represents an hundred and eighty degree turn from his pro-Mormon stance in those earlier years when Utah was frantically petitioning for statehood and territorial status. But in the

[1]The Douglas speech was published in full in the *Missouri Republican,* June 18, 1857.

year previous (1856) the Republican Party had sprung into existence. John C. Fremont was its first presidential candidate. The new party's platform—territorial prohibition of "those twin relics of barbarism—polygamy and slavery"—could scarcely have been better timed or more prophetic of events to come. The Utah Expedition, and Mr. Douglas's inflammatory bombast were deliberately calculated by the administration to remind American voters that the Democrats had just as ready an answer to the nation's clamor.

It would yet be said, before the affair was over, that armed intervention in Utah constituted an overt move to scatter U.S. forces prior to the Confederate rebellion; the entire adventure would be called a "contractors' war" when its freighting cost of 22 cents a pound were added up; and it would be labeled "Buchanan's blunder." But now, in the clarion call of Stephen A. Douglas, and the rumble of supply trains out of Fort Leavenworth westward, it meant nothing less than undeclared war and hostile invasion to Utah and the Mormons.

TROOPS ON THE MOVE

First positive steps in forming the "Expedition" had been taken May 27, 1857 in general orders of the War Department for the "gathering of a body of troops at Fort Leavenworth, to march to Utah as soon as assembled."[2] It is astonishing that an operation of such magnitude could have been carried forward in such secrecy. Because of the government's abrupt shut-off of all mail westward to Salt Lake Valley, the Mormons themselves were tardiest of all in learning of the movement so dramatically astir.

[2]See *House Executive Documents*, 35th Congress, No. 71, pp. 4-5.

FORT BRIDGER—LATER SITE OF CAMP SCOTT

—From an old print.

It remained for the last eastbound Utah mail, under aegis of Brigham's "YX Company," to intercept troops and supply trains moving westward over the plains. Abraham O. Smoot, mayor of Salt Lake City, in bringing this last mail eastward, ran head-on into a detachment of U.S. cavalry. Later, an hundred miles west of Independence, this now thoroughly alarmed Utah citizen intercepted heavy laden army supply trains, whose escorts and teamsters, on inquiries, were suspiciously reticent about naming their destination.

In Independence Smoot learned that the Mormon mail not only had been arbitrarily suspended, but that the contract with "YX" had been cancelled by the government. It took only a little discreet inquiry to realize the scope of the military operations afoot. Smoot had no alternative. He must return to Utah with utmost haste. And, in his warning flight westward, he must break up all YX mail stations en route.

On the plains the returning Smoot party, driving their mail stock before them, intercepted Orrin Porter Rockwell with July's eastbound mail from Utah. Leaving stock and equipment to others in the party, the two men continued westward under forced drive, arriving in Salt Lake City July 23, 1857.

Brigham Young, they quickly learned, with most of local Mormondom, was celebrating the tenth anniversary of the Pioneers' entrance into Salt Lake Valley. The celebrants had chosen Big Cottonwood Canyon as scene of festivities. Smoot and Rockwell sped their horses canyonward. In midst of the 24th of July celebration, the dramatic news of the advancing army was made known to Governor Young and the Saints.

The expedition did not clear Fort Leavenworth in one body or in anything resembling grand martial style. General W. S. Harney, as commander, did not take up the line of march with the first units, but remained at Leavenworth to argue out the wisdom of launching a military adventure into the Rocky Mountains with summer already half gone.

But the great supply trains—wheeled by civilian contractors and guarded by small army units—were already kicking the Kansas dust westward. And, on July 18, the first of the army's fighting strength was taking itself to the field. There was no lack of enthusiasm in the ranks. The goal—chastisement of Brigham and his Mormon rebels—outweighed any physical hazards of the long march.

Captain Jesse A. Gove, of the 10th Infantry, could thus write to his wife in far-away New Hampshire, on the eve of his first day afield: "It is Sunday, and the sun is just setting in the west. As night approaches I think of you the more, as the weary day's march is done. Well, my dear Maria, we are on our way to Utah . . . The 10th Inf., notwithstanding the old woman[3] at the head, is one of the best regiments in the service. I am proud to be associated with so many gallant men. It would have done your heart good to have seen them break up their camp last evening about 6 P.M. to take up its line of march as the advance of Gen. Harney's army to march on Utah. It is complimentary to the 10th that they lead the van . . . In all about 600 men when they passed Gen. Harney's quarters in the Fort, band playing and Col. Smith in command. It was a splendid sight. We marched about 8 miles to Salt Creek

[3]Gove's private cognomen for Colonel Edmund B. Alexander.

and encamped . . . Today we have marched about 10 miles. It is intended to make these gradual marches through to Utah. . . . I can assure you that it makes a very warlike appearance to see our command moving along the road. Phelp's battery follows tomorrow, then the 5th Inf., then 2nd Dragoons . . ."[4]

On July 20 Captain Gove recorded: "Here we are in camp, the third day of our pilgrimage to (not the Holy Land) the Mormon bedlam, in a ravine surrounded on either side by rolling bluffs, while to the right lies the little creek, wooded, to which or on we have encamped. Our march was short today on account of water . . . We have a very large train besides the regimental trains; they are our supplies. As we come along, to look back and see them winding along behind the column is a sight that pleases the eye of all romance lovers. . . . Today I had the front. Band goes ahead of the column but conforms to the leading company. Today front, tomorrow rear. Such is the clock work of military movements . . .

"The 'old woman' joined us last night; got in his ambulance and I hope he will keep there. Col. Smith is ordered to stay at Leavenworth. Col. Canby has the direction of everything, and a more attentive, careful officer never strode a horse . . ."[5]

The men now in the field, Captain Gove included, could scarcely be fully informed of all the factors now integrating themselves into the great undertaking. The 1st Cavalry and all units of the 6th Infantry, stationed at Fort Laramie, had been issued their orders to join the expedition. At Fort Kearney, an entire new slate of civil officers for Utah, including Alfred Cumming (to replace

[4]Gove, Capt. Jesse A., *The Utah Expedition, 1857-1858,* Letters of Capt. Jesse A. Gove, 10th Inf., U.S.A. New Hampshire Historical Society.

[5]*Ibid.*

the "rebellious" Brigham Young as territorial governor), joined their entourage with the military. Traveling with the group of civilian authorities were their wives, including Mrs. Cumming, wife of the new governor. No one imagined but what entrance into Utah, in view of the army's overwhelming strength, would be the simple and easy thing Buchanan and the War Department had anticipated.

Captain Gove, in a letter from Fort Kearney, makes casual mention of the advance party, under orders of the military, to push on to Utah ahead of the troops—the detachment on general quartermaster scout, that the army might be safely winter-quartered in the Valley of the Saints. "Today or yesterday rather [August 9, 1857], Captain Van Vliet, quartermaster's department, arrived by express, under orders to go to Utah in 25 days, has an escort from the 10th Inf. of one officer (Lt. Deshler), 1 sergt. (Preston), 1 corporal and 28 privates, to go in wagons. Leave tomorrow. I furnish sergt. and five men . . ."[6]

It is generally believed that General Harney never was in complete sympathy with the administration's military adventure against the Mormons in Utah. Whether or not this attitude precipitated his dismissal as commander of the expedition is a matter for conjecture, but the fact remains that Harney never left Leavenworth to take up duties with his troops on the march. The matter of command, until the army reached the Rockies, devolved almost entirely upon fussy and befuddled Colonel B. Alexander, the "old woman" of the expedition.

Appointment of Captain Stewart Van Vliet for a fast excursion westward ahead of the main body of troops, with special instructions for a conference with Governor

[6] *Ibid.*, p. 31.

Brigham Young as to the army's intents and purposes, was one of Harney's last acts before relinquishing command to Albert Sidney Johnston. The orders, written by Captain Pleasanton, assistant adjutant general to General Harney, very plainly briefed Van Vliet on the purpose of his presence in the land of the "rebellious Saints."

THE VAN VLIET EXPRESS

First of all, Van Vliet was to negotiate with the Mormons for the encampment and provisioning of the expedition, and "that the general commanding has deemed it proper and courteous to inform President Young, of the society of Mormons, of the object of your visit, and has also requested of him the required facilities to enable you to execute your instruction certainly and effectively . . .

"You will obtain a suitable location for the troops in the vicinity of Salt Lake City, sufficiently near to be effective in supporting the civil authority in the maintenance of the territorial laws, but allowing ample room to prevent an improper association of the troops with the citizens—an object in this selection of primary importance . . .

"You will impress upon the officers in charge of your escort the imperious necessity for a very careful circumspection of conduct in his command. The men should not only be carefully selected for this service, but they should be repeatedly admonished never to comment upon or ridicule anything they may either see or hear, and to treat the inhabitants of Utah with kindness and consideration."[7]

At least General Harney could not be accused of planning a campaign of revenge and destruction against the Mormon people.

[7] *Senate Documents*, 35th Congress, 1st session, vol. iii, pp. 27-28.

But, after Harney's dismissal, command of the Utah Expedition was assigned to General Persifer F. Smith. Before General Smith, however, could move a mile westward to take his official place with the marching columns, he fell desperately ill at Fort Leavenworth, and died before ever having assumed field command. Colonel (later General) Albert Sidney Johnston became final choice as leader, and to this austere and efficient soldier went full responsibility for successful conduct of the campaign.

Not until the chill of winter, and deepest misfortune had settled upon a mountain-stranded army, did Johnston finally reach the side of his beleagured fellow officers and men. There, winterbound, he took over personal direction of the immense and difficult task so abruptly handed him.

VIII

Utah Goes to War

MORMONS have always considered it climactic that first realization of the imminent "invasion" of Utah occurred at the precise time when the Saints were celebrating the tenth anniversary of their entrance into the great valley. Here, forever, was to have been their rendezvous and sanctuary. Here, it was expected, they would find religious liberty and secure haven from the mobocratic oppression they had suffered in Ohio, Missouri, and Illinois.

Two thousand Utah families had been tendered personal invitations by Governor Brigham Young to participate in a gigantic picnic to be held at the headwaters of Big Cottonwood Creek, in the picturesque and rugged canyon of that name. It would be a three-day affair, with the major festivities scheduled for July 24—the anniversary date.

As early as July 22 the celebrants began to arrive at the shores of Silver Lake, the picnic site in the canyon. "By good time in the afternoon all the company, numbering 2,587 persons with 464 carriages and wagons, 1,028 horses and mules and 332 oxen and cows, were encamped and busily engaged in their several arrangements for the morrow.

"Captain Bello's Band, the Nauvoo Brass Band, the Springville Brass Band, and the Great Salt Lake City and the Ogden City martial bands were in attendance; also the 1st company of light artillery, under the command of Adjt. Gen. James Ferguson, a detachment of four platoons of Life Guards and one platoon of the Lancers under the command of Col. R. T. Burton, and one company of light infantry under the command of Captain John W. Young...

"At 4 p.m. the Martial Bands serenaded the camp.

"At sunset notes from a bugle summoned the Saints to an eminence near the centre of the camp ground, when Pres. Brigham Young made a few remarks, recounting the mercies of God to this people in delivering them from the power of their enemies, in making the desert places blossom like the rose and the sterile plains yield luscious fruits and golden grain, in loading the leaves of the trees and shrubbery with honey dew and in increasing our flocks and herds in a marvelous manner. . . . Heber C. Kimball offered a prayer of thanksgiving unto God for his goodness to his people, prayed for Israel and Israel's enemies, and renewedly dedicated and consecrated unto God the ground, the waters, the timbers, the rocks and all the elements pertaining to the stream whose head waters we were assembled to celebrate the 10th anniversary of the entrance of the pioneer into these valleys.

"Three spacious boweries, with plank floors, had been provided . . . and a large number passed the evening in joyous dance.

"On July 24th, each one began to enjoy the privileges of the occasion as best suited their several tastes and feelings, in accordance with the order of the day . . .

"The different bands played at intervals throughout the day, and greatly added to the zest of the varied sources of enjoyment . . .

"The Stars and Stripes were unfurled on two of the highest peaks in sight of the camp and on the tops of two of the tallest trees.

"At 20 minutes past nine a.m. three rounds were fired from a brass howitzer, for the First Presidency of the Church of Jesus Christ of Latter-day Saints and our rights and independence . . .

"At about sunset the camp assembled for prayers, when President [Daniel H.] Wells made a few remarks in relation to the latest tidings from the States . . ."[1]

The "few remarks" of Daniel H. Wells, Mormon militia general, was a disclosure to the Saints of the first reports of the American Army's movement westward. Governor Young was at that very moment closeted with the three weary travelers—Abraham O. Smoot, Orrin Porter Rockwell and Judson Stoddard—who had made a forced drive of 513 miles in five days from Fort Laramie. They had arrived in Salt Lake City the previous evening, only to find Young absent from the city.

"About noon [July 24] Messrs. Smoot, Stoddard and Rockwell, these men with the 'war news,' accompanied by Judge Elias Smith from Salt Lake City, rode in upon this scene of peace and joy and patriotism. Their advent, however, did not disturb the peace and joyousness of the occasion. Their message was delivered quietly to President Young and his immediate counselors and associates. For the rest, the afternoon's merriment went on as if no messengers from the east had arrived."[2]

[1]*Deseret News*, issue of July 29, 1857.

[2]Roberts, *Comprehensive History*, vol. IV, p. 237.

DANIEL H. WELLS
Commander of Utah's "Nauvoo Legion"
—From *Contributor*, Vol. IX.

According to these three couriers of bad tidings, Feramorz Little had been the first to penetrate governmental secrecy regarding the expedition. Little, while serving as mail representative for the Utah operated YX Company at Independence, had heard considerable talk among contractors hoping to grab some of the lush freighting assignments for hauling an enormous amount of military supplies westward, presumably to Utah. On June 1 Little had left Independence with the accumulated Salt Lake mail, and with a gnawing conviction that a move for armed intervention was actually under way.

At Fort Laramie, Little intercepted Abraham Smoot, headed east with Utah's June mail. Little told Smoot of what he had learned. Between Fort Laramie and Fort Kearney, Smoot ran into several hundred United States troops, whose commander offered him military escort into Kearney. This offer Smoot declined. The great supply trains of William R. Russell, heavily loaded with military freight, were encountered one hundred miles west of Independence. The drivers were reticent about revealing their destination, but Smoot's suspicions, along with Feramorz Little's findings, were quickly verified on Smoot's arrival at Independence. Here Smoot was formally notified of the cancellation of the YX Company's mail contract.

All he could do now was break up the company's stations and move the stock westward. The Utah-bound Smoot party met O. P. Rockwell, with Salt Lake's July mail, 120 miles east of Fort Laramie. Acting on the facts at hand, the men then started their frenzied dash westward, bearing the news of the army's approach. At the Big Cottonwood picnic Brigham Young was made rudely and grimly aware of what lay ahead for him and his people.

Though the feasting and the music went on scarcely disturbed by the tragic disclosure, Brigham Young now moved with speed and precision. There is ample evidence, however, that Brigham had delayed this "sudden disclosure" until it suited him to effectively and dramatically announce it. Smoot and Rockwell were not the first to warn him that an army was on the march. It seems certain that the fact had been revealed to him many weeks before the anniversary celebration at Big Cottonwood. The Mormon leader had simply waited for more definite confirmation, and had chosen the most effective time and place to drop the bombshell.

Mormon militia, previously and carefully reorganized by Lieut. General Daniel H. Wells, were immediately alerted. Certainly, when the Saints returned to Salt Lake City, cognizance was everywhere made of this new and terrible threat to their existence. A warlike atmosphere had supplanted the peace and merriment of their anniversary celebration.

PREPARATION FOR HOSTILITIES

There could be no doubting the Saints contemplated vigorous defense of their Zion. To Utah's militia—or Nauvoo Legion, as it still was known—General Wells issued official orders August 1, 1857.

The people of Utah had lived, the order reminded, "in strict obedience to the laws of the parent and home government, and are zealous for the supremacy of the Constitution and the rights guaranteed thereby;" but "in such times, when anarchy takes the place of orderly government, and mobocratic tyranny usurps the power of rulers," the people "have left the inalienable right to defend themselves against all aggression upon their constitutional privileges."[3]

Mormons justified resistance in that for "successive years" the Saints had witnessed the desolation of their homes, the barbarous wrath of mobs poured upon their unoffending brethren, their leaders arrested, incarcerated and slain, and themselves driven to cull life from the desert. District commanders were instructed to hold their troops in readiness, and "as far as practicable, that each ten [men] be provided with a good wagon and four horses or mules as well as necessary clothing, etc., for a winter campaign. . . . *Avoid all excitement, but be ready.*"[4]

Next step was to call all apostles in from their worldwide missions. Outlying Mormon settlements, such as Carson Valley, San Bernardino, and Idaho, were ordered broken up. Saints, wherever they might be, were expected to return home to aid in the defense of Zion.

Brigham Young now followed with moves even more drastic and warlike. Acting as territorial governor, he dispatched Samuel W. Richards to Washington, D.C., to inform President Buchanan, through Colonel Thomas L. Kane, that the American Army *could not* enter Utah until satisfactory arrangements had been made on executive commission level. After dropping the scorching missive in the hands of Colonel Kane for transmission to the President, Richards hurried on to Europe to supervise the return of all Mormon leaders from overseas.

Kane, sympathetic as always toward the Mormons, loyally interceded in their behalf—though wording of Brigham's memorial could scarcely be calculated to cement friendship in this hour of crisis. Its carping on the

[3]Roberts, *Comprehensive History,* vol. IV, p. 239.

[4]The order is given *extenso* in *Contributor,* vol. III, p. 177.

offensiveness of territorial appointees indicates even Governor Young was not yet fully cognizant of the magnitude of the government's reprisal against his Saints.

But Brigham's protest was scorchingly angry in tone: "If you intend to continue the appointment of certain officers, we respectfully suggest that you appoint actually intelligent and honorable men, who will wisely attend to their own duties, and send them unaccompanied by troops, which you yourself know are of no lawful use here—and your officers will be treated strictly according to their acts and merits, as you also well know has always been the case, except that we did not hang up some of the infernal scoundrels you have heretofore sent, as they most richly deserved. And if you will not receive this fair counsel, but persist in sending us officials from the tag, rag and bobtail of whore houses, grog shops and gambling hells, we shall take the yankee liberty . . . for the first time of using up that class of officials strictly in accordance with their deserts."[5]

UTAH IN THE FIELD

Utah forces were in the field as early as August 15, 1857. A "corps of observation" under command of Legion Colonel Robert T. Burton moved eastward, ostensibly to protect Mormon migration on the plains, though in reality to learn the strength and disposition of the oncoming troops, and to report their progress to headquarters in Salt Lake City.

Another company, under Captain Andrew Cunningham, was sent to Fort Hall vicinity to guard the northern approaches into Zion. Colonel C. W. West's group was deployed to watch the Bear River entrance.

[5]Roberts, *Comprehensive History*, vol. IV, p. 244.

Before August was out Burton and his men had intercepted a large government supply train near Fort Bridger, and by September 8, Colonel Alexander's division of the United States Army was under constant surveillance (5th and 10th infantry regiments, Phelps' battery, and Reno's battery). Not only was Mormon headquarters in Salt Lake City apprised of their movement, but they were trailed every mile to their encampment at Ham's Fork.

Up to now Brigham Young and his fully aroused Saints had been of the opinion General W. S. Harney was in supreme command of the expedition. One of the first things learned from the field, however, was that Harney had remained in Kansas, and that General—then Colonel—Albert Sidney Johnston had been put in charge. And by now they were fully aware that "soldier talk" from Ham's Fork to Leavenworth was of little else than what the army intended doing to the "Goddamned Mormons" once they arrived in Salt Lake Valley.

They learned too that Captain Stewart Van Vliet, with a small detachment, was speeding on to Utah to commandeer or negotiate for supplies and camping space for the expedition.

CHARACTER OF THE ARMY

It was only natural that Mormons, steeped in bitter memories of their forced expulsion from Illinois and Missouri at point of bayonet, should look upon the suddenly appearing Utah Expedition as deepest sort of threat to their peace and security, if not a sure and certain omen to their destruction.

Heavy comparisons are made in Mormon literature and news items of that period, between Johnston's Army and the "accursed mobs" and traitorous militia the Saints had faced ten years previous. Actually, even in their belliger-

LONG LINES OF FEDERAL TROOPS WINDING WESTWARD TOWARD UTAH

—*Frank Leslie's Illustrated Newspaper*, Jan. 8, 1859.

ence and defiance, the Saints in the fall of 1857, appear to have grossly underestimated the strength and character of their foe. And, since the government inexplicably refused to make known to Utah the true purpose of the expedition, the army's appearance was interpreted by them as war and invasion rather than occupational in character.

Ribaldry and camp threats of Alexander's advance divisions could very well have given color to Brigham's claim of an "armed, mercenary mob," but in truth Johnston's Army was the very flower of America's military might. Roster of its officers include many of the brightest names in military history.

This flowering of military might included such legendary names as General W. S. Harney—seasoned campaigner who had, among other accomplishments, mercilessly defeated the Brule Sioux at Ash Hollow; General Albert Sidney Johnston, proud and inflexible Kentuckian, graduate of West Point, destined to be the never-to-be-forgotten hero of Shiloh, where he would meet death as a Confederate general; General Fitz John Porter, son of a distinguished American family, and an officer who was to serve with distinction in the Union Army through that same Civil War to come; Colonel E. B. Alexander, an efficient and gentlemanly officer; Lieutenant Colonel Charles F. Smith, another West Pointer, had already distinguished himself in every great battle of the Mexican War, and later would be the Civil War hero of the capture of Fort Donelson, and for a time actually supersede General Ulysses Grant in command; Captain Stewart Van Vliet, a mild and kindly man, who later would rise in rank to Major General; Colonel (later Major General) Philip St. George Cooke, commanding six companies of Second Dragoons, was that same beloved leader of the Mormon

Battalion on its historic western march in the Mexican War, and who would rise to high distinction in the Civil War; Captain Randolph Barnes Marcy (later Brigadier General) a graduate of West Point, who would become chief of staff to General McClellan in the Civil War, and later to author many books on the great west.

In general, it was a magnificent army, and well officered in spite of its hasty planning, and the obscurity of its motives. Tragedy is that Mormons were never made conscious of the fact that the army could have had any other intention than fighting its way into Utah.

That the commanders themselves were devoid of any clear-cut idea of the expedition's purpose is demonstrated by Van Vliet's embarrassment on his arrival in Salt Lake City, September 8. Immediately he closeted himself with Brigham Young and the Mormon leaders, at Social Hall. To every anxious question put to him by the Saints, as to the army's real intent, he could give only haziest of answers. His job, he pointed out, was strictly a quartermaster assignment—to locate a suitable base camp; to arrange for the purchase of food, lumber, and supplies. What the military planned to do with Brigham and his Saints, Van Vliet claimed no official knowledge.

Without assurance even from this advance detachment, Brigham quickly drew his own conclusions as to the army's plan and purpose. Men in the field had listened to the braggadocio around the army's campfires, as to what was in store for the Saints. Returning missionaries from the east and Europe had amply unburdened themselves as to the anti-Mormon howlings of America's press and pulpit. Johnston's troops were coming as an army of conquest. This army would be met by Mormons as an invading enemy.

Brigham haughtily assured Van Vliet the Saints had food, supplies and lumber in abundance, but none whatever would be issued or sold to the enemy. If Johnston's Army planned a base camp in the vales of Zion, they would have to fight for it. And, in the day it was won, the invaders would find a Utah as devastated of life and habitation as Mormons themselves had found it.

Van Vliet was an impressed and chastened man on his return to the east. Accompanying him, bound for Washington, was Dr. John M. Bernhisel, Utah's territorial representative to Congress. At South Pass, the men intercepted Alexander's command, and other advance units of the American Army. Van Vliet's solemn advice was for these units, under penalty of bloodshed, not to attempt a force of passage into Utah.

Commanders and men, bent on mixing it with Zion's Saints, treated Van Vliet's morbid predictions with a good deal of facetiousness. But the captain knew, as Alexander was soon to know, that invasion of Utah would be no simple military exercise.

MORMONS TAKE WAR TO THE ENEMY

Van Vliet had departed Salt Lake City on September 15. The day following, Brigham Young, as territorial governor of Utah, flung out his now-famous proclamation of martial law:

> We are invaded by a hostile force who are evidently assailing us to accomplish our overthrow and destruction.
>
> For the last twenty-five years we have trusted officials of the government, from constables and justices to judges, governors and presidents, only to be scorned, held in derision, insulted and betrayed. Our houses have been plundered and then burned, our fields laid waste, our principal men butchered while under the pledged faith of the government for their

safety, and our families driven from their homes to find that shelter in the barren wilderness and that protection among hostile savages, which were denied them in the boasted abodes of christianity and civilization.

The Constitution of our common country guarantees unto us all that we do now, or have ever claimed. If the constitutional rights which pertain unto us as American citizens were extended to Utah, according to the spirit and meaning thereof, and fairly and impartially administered, it is all that we could ask, all that we have ever asked.

Our opponents have availed themselves of prejudices existing against us because of our religious faith, to send out a formidable host to accomplish our destruction. We have had no privilege, no opportunity of defending ourselves from the false, foul, and unjust aspersions against us before the nation. The government has not condescended to cause an investigation committee or other persons to be sent to inquire into and ascertain the truth, as is customary in such cases.

We know these aspersions to be false, but that avails us nothing. We are condemned unheard and forced to an issue with an armed, mercenary mob, which has been sent against us at the instigation of anonymous letter writers ashamed to father the base, slanderous falsehoods which they have given to the public; of corrupt officials who have brought false accusations against us to screen themselves in their own infamy; and of hireling priests and howling editors who prostitute the truth for filthy lucre's sake.

The issue which has been thus forced upon us compels us to resort to the great first law of self-preservation . . .

Our duty to ourselves, to our families, requires us not to tamely submit to be driven and slain, without an attempt to preserve ourselves . . .

Therefore, I, Brigham Young, governor, and superintendent of Indian affairs for the territory of Utah, in the name of the people of the United States in the territory of Utah,

1st—Forbid all armed forces, of every description, from coming into this territory under any pretense whatever.

2nd—That all the forces in said territory hold themselves in readiness to march, at a moment's notice, to repel any and all such invasion.

3rd—Martial law is hereby declared to exist in this territory, from and after the publication of this proclamation; and no person shall be allowed to pass or repass into, or through or from this territory, without a permit from the proper officer.[6]

Twelve hundred and fifty men of the territorial militia ["Nauvoo Legion"] were immediately ordered to Echo Canyon, as do-or-die guardians of Zion's portals. Their officers were prayed over, and individually "set apart" to holy duty by Mormon "laying on of hands." Next move was for General Daniel Wells to deliver to Colonel Edmund B. Alexander, U.S.A., an ultimatum from Brigham. It was classically phrased:

I am still the governor and superintendent of Indian affairs for this territory, and no successor having been appointed and qualified, as provided by law; nor have I been removed by the president of the United States.

By virtue of the authority thus vested in me, I have issued, and forwarded you a copy of my proclamation forbidding the entrance of armed forces into this territory. This you have disregarded. I now further direct that you retire forthwith from the territory, by the same route you entered . . .[7]

Colonel Alexander politely replied that his troops were there by orders of the President of the United States, and that their future movements would depend upon "orders issued by competent authority"—which did not include those of Brigham Young.

With Alexander's rebuff, the war started for Mormons in earnest. In night-riding guerrilla bands they took the fight directly to the "enemy" by stampeding government stock, and continuous harassment of supply trains.

In combatting these tactics, Alexander's forces were only partially successful. Their first minor victory was to

[6]*House Executive Documents*, 35th Congress, 1st session, X, No. 71, pp. 34-35.

[7]*House Executive Documents*, 35th Congress, 1st Session, X, No. 71, p. 33.

capture a group of Mormon riders under command of Militia Major Joseph Taylor. In Taylor's possession were incriminating orders from Daniel Wells to Utah troops in the field, revealing to the American military a few of the things they could expect from the rebellious Saints. From Wells' letters of instructions it made clear that Mormons were to harass the moving army continuously, to stampede their animals, to burn the supply trains, and to set afire every blade of forage grass ahead of the expedition.

P.S.—If the troops have not passed, or have turned in this direction, follow their rear, and continue to annoy them, burning any trains they may leave. Take no life, but destroy their trains, and stampede or drive away their animals at every opportunity. D. H. WELLS.[8]

The army was not long in suffering literal fulfillment of these instructions. On October 3, 1857 Fort Bridger and Fort Supply both vanished under flames from Mormon torches. Every spear of grass surrounding or ahead of the advancing columns was consumed to the scorched earth by the rolling flames deliberately set by the raiders.

When Fort Bridger and Fort Supply were nothing but heaps of glowing ashes, Wells ordered Major Lot Smith to take a company of men and intercept the supply trains then advancing from South Pass, and "either turn them back or burn them."

First prize to the Mormon raiders was the fat westward-headed train in charge of a Captain Rankin. Lot Smith brazenly informed the surprised Rankin that it would be healthier for him and his men if he turned the train about, and headed back to the States.

"By what authority?" Rankin asked

[8]Captured document copied *extenso* into *House Executive Documents*, 35th Congress, 1st session, X, No. 71, pp. 56-57.

Smith pointed to his sober and belligerent Mormons hidden in the brush.

Rankin was prudent enough to take the hint without further resistance. He turned his bull-train and headed it back toward Fort Leavenworth. It was reported that he later claimed to have reversed direction when Mormons were well out of sight. But, by then, Lot Smith and his guerrillas were in hot pursuit of the mules from the 10th Regiment.

Under cover of darkness, with only 23 men, Smith's band swooped down on one train of 52 wagons encamped for the night about their fires. Shrewdly keeping a number of his riders concealed in the shadows, that sentries might have no accurate idea as to size of the attacking force, Smith and a picked squad of his men, guns drawn, boldly strode into the firelight. To the startled leader, a Captain Dawson, Smith announced his intention of applying the torch.

"For God's sake don't burn the trains!" Dawson protested.

"It's for His sake I *am* going to burn them," Smith answered.

The camp was disarmed, the weapons stacked, and the men put under guard. Oddly, in midst of the raid, a courier arrived from Colonel Alexander warning Dawson that "Mormons were in the field; that captains and teamsters must not go to sleep; that four companies of cavalry and two pieces of artillery would arrive in the morning."[9]

When the Mormons retreated to the Green River bluffs, they left behind nothing but charred remnants of 51 wagonloads of precious military freight. The sole remain-

[9]"Lot Smith's Narrative in Echo Canyon War," Wells, *Contributor*, vol. III, p. 273.

ing wagon housed the personals of the unhappy Dawson and his men.

Two nights later, on the Big Sandy, Mormons intercepted another train of 25 wagons, at a point known since as Simpson's Hollow. Again the raiders allowed its Captain Simpson and teamsters to load up two of the wagons with personal clothing and provisions. All remaining vehicles were burned.

Smith: "I want your pistols."

Simpson: "By God, sir, no man ever took them yet. If you think you can, without killing me, try it."

Smith: "I admire a brave man. I don't like blood. You insist on my killing you—which will only take a minute. I don't want to do it."

Simpson: "You have me at a disadvantage. My men are disarmed."

Smith: "What will you do if I give them back their arms?"

Simpson: "Fight you, by God!"

Smith: "We know something about that, too. Take up your arms, men!"

Men (in chorus): "Not by a damned sight! We came out here to whack bulls, not to fight Mormons!"[10]

According to the congressional *House Documents,* these Mormon fire parties were disastrous to the advancing army. Records show that the burnings consumed 2,720 pounds of ham; 92,700 pounds of bacon; 167,900 pounds of flour; 8,580 pounds of coffee; 13,333 pounds of soap; 68,832 rations of dessicated vegetables; 7,781 pounds of hard bread; 25,000 pounds of various other food supplies.

Few shots were fired in the ghostlike forays, and so far as is known, no one was killed. But Colonel Alexander was forced by these exigencies into what was virtually a calamitous defeat.

[10]*Ibid.,* vol. IV, pp. 27-28.

All hope of getting the advance units through the mountains into Utah had to be abandoned. Winter quarters were set up at Ham's Fork, on the Green River. No grass remained for the starving animals; rations issued troops and teamsters were scarcely enough to keep bodies alive. Winter was setting in. Rocky Mountain blizzards had already sealed the passes into Zion. And they etched a pattern of horror for the famished, half-frozen troops under Alexander's command.

On October 28, amidst this misery, General Albert Sidney Johnston arrived at Ham's Fork. With Johnston came additional forces, and a few desperately needed supply trains. His appearance infused new hope into the now badly demoralized army.

The commander took one look at the winterbound camp, and ordered its removal forthwith to the ruins of Fort Bridger. Temperature was fifteen degrees below zero. So badly were men and animals spent that it took fifteen days for them to go thirty-five miles.

On November 15, Colonel P. St. George Cooke arrived, with six companies of the Second Dragoons, and the civil officers to take over the Territory of Utah from Brigham Young and the Mormon hierarchy. On arrival at Bridger, Cooke had his own tale of suffering. Two-thirds of his animals had perished en route. "It has been of starvation; the earth has a no more lifeless, treeless, grassless desert; it contains scarcely a wolf to glut itself on the hundreds of dead and frozen animals which for thirty miles block the road; with abandoned and shattered property, they mark, perhaps, beyond example in history, the steps of an advancing army with the horrors of a disastrous retreat."[11]

[11]*House Executive Documents,* 35th Congress, 1st session, X, No. 71, pp. 92-93.

Knowing that King Winter had effectively allied himself to their cause, and that Johnston's Army was hopelessly trapped until spring thaw, the Mormons withdrew their forces to Salt Lake Valley—maintaining garrisons only at the canyon approaches to their Zion.

During that bitter winter Brigham Young made several offers of food to the starving soldiers, only to be rebuffed by the straitlaced and unbending Johnston. Final overture on Brigham's part was the dispatching of a load of salt. It received quick and churlish rejection.

For there was no love in Johnston's heart for the rebellious Saints. He had with him a long winter in which to nurse grievances for the predicament of his troops, and to plan his revenge. "Occupying as they do, an attitude of rebellion and open defiance to the government, connected with numerous overt acts of treason," he wrote, "I have ordered that when they are met in arms, that they be treated as enemies."[12]

There is something ironical, especially to Mormons, in the fact that Johnston was later to die at Shiloh, in open rebellion against the very government he was so determined to defend against the rebel Saints.

[12]Johnston's letters to Major Irvine McDowell, assistant adjutant general, headquarters, U.S. Army.

IX

The Smoke and Flame of Politics

DURING that winter of 1857 there were two active capitals of Utah Territory—Salt Lake City, and Camp Winfield Scott (formerly Fort Bridger).

From Camp Scott, Alfred Cumming, Buchanan's appointee to fill the office of territorial governor in place of Brigham Young, issued a wordy proclamation to the people of Utah. This first official pronouncement, in general, covered the following points:

1—That he (Cumming) had been appointed July 11, 1857 by the President of the United States.

2—That he would proceed to Salt Lake City as soon as possible, but in the meantime he would make preliminary arrangements for the reorganization of the territory.

3—That proceedings would be instituted at Camp Scott against "those in rebellion," presided over by Chief Justice (D. R.) Eckels.

4—That the Utah people were promised "a just and firm administration."

5—That all Mormons bearing arms were ordered to immediately disband and return to their homes.[1]

[1]The Cumming paper is included in *House Executive Documents*, 1st session, X, No. 71, p. 76.

Brigham Young and "sixty of his principal associates" were indicted for treason by a grand jury made up of army teamsters and camp followers. Other indictments, laws and resolutions in behalf of the territory the appointees had not yet reached to govern, flowed out of Camp Scott's extraordinary body of lawmakers.

In the meantime the regular Utah legislature continued in session at Salt Lake City. Petitions from this territorial legislature went out to Congress for a withdrawal of the army; for redress of the wrongs allegedly heaped upon the citizens of Utah. On January 12, 1858, a great mass meeting was held in Salt Lake City. Memorials were excitedly prepared for Congress and the President of the United States:

"We call upon you to reconsider your acts, to mete out to us even-handed justice, to withdraw your army, restore our mails, execute justice upon our oppressors, and give us our constitutional rights. We ask no more, but that, in the name of God, we will have, He being our helper . . .

". . . Our voice is the united voice of nearly one hundred thousand Americans, laboring under the most unprecedented cruelty, outrage and wrongs . . ."[2]

In spite of peril, the atmosphere of Utah during the winter of 1857-58 was outwardly one of jubilance and self-confidence. Mormons were proud of the way the Lord had acted in their behalf by putting the army of the Philistines in cold storage for the winter. Israel had been victorious. Of this there could be no denying.

And yet, beneath it all, Governor Young and the leaders were becoming increasingly aware their victory was but a temporary one. Johnston definitely meant business. As a commander he was known to be dogged and tenacious in pursuance of an objective.

[2]*Deseret News,* issue of Jan. 27, 1858.

Brigham was insistent that resistance, martial law, and warlike preparations were necessary to counter an hostile invasion. Repeatedly he declared he had been tendered no official notification of his displacement as governor, nor of the assignment of federal troops to the territory; that he had no recourse other than to regard the army as a punitive invasion. He was certain that Buchanan expected Mormons to oppose the troops. There were obscure political reasons for generating military hostility in the far west to forestall the divisive states' rights ferment which was gripping the nation. The secrecy in which the whole movement was cloaked; the absence of any attempt to seek congressional approval for the venture; the discontinuance of mail service; and, above all, the failure to communicate with him as territorial governor as to intent and purposes, were totally indicative of undeclared war. Mormons had no alternative other than to fight for their homeland.

So, all of Utah Territory labored under martial law. Saints from every distant colony were called home to Zion's defense. The territorial militia, known from Illinois days as the Nauvoo Legion, was mustered into full-time service. General Daniel H. Wells commanded three thousand able men in his bucolic force—a rather ragged lot, and armed with every conceivable type of weapon, but fired with total zeal known only to a religious war.

A STRATEGY BORN OF FEAR

The Corps of Observation, a mounted force of less than an hundred men had, in the fall, been sent to scout the invading army, protect and aid the Mormon immigrants on the plains, and locate strategic points to intercept and harass the advancing troops. Fifty more men, known as the "Blackfoot Fork Mission" had been detailed to scout the northern route of the Utah Expedition. Another detachment of mounted raiders, consisting of more than 100 seasoned plains veterans had, under command of Major Lot Smith, already played havoc with Alexander's advance forces.

"On ascertaining the locality or route of the troops, proceed at once to annoy them in every possible way. Use every exertion to stampede their animals, and set fire to their trains. Burn the whole country before them and on their flanks. Keep them from sleeping by night surprises. Blockade the road by felling trees, or destroying the fords when you can. Watch for opportunities to set fire to the grass on their windward, so as, if possible, to envelop their trains. Leave no grass before them . . . Take no life, but destroy their trains, and stampede or drive away their animals, at every opportunity."[3]

And as U.S. troops had drawn ever closer to their objective, the task forces already raiding the supply trains and columns on the plains had been strengthened by the moving into Echo Canyon of Nauvoo Legion's main defensive force of approximately 1,200 men—known as the Easten Expedition. They would bear the brunt of fighting should Johnston decide to broach the mountain gates leading into Salt Lake Valley.

Militiamen of the Eastern Expedition had been recruited from the Utah communities, and locally outfitted with clothing, boots, blankets, food and guns. Mormon outposts, such as San Bernardino in California, and Carson Valley in Nevada, had been ordered to contribute all they could in arms and ammunition. San Bernardino had

[3]Orders, signed by Daniel H. Wells, dated Oct. 4, 1857, found in possession of Maj. Joseph Taylor when captured by U.S. troops. *House Executive Documents,* No. 71, -57.

GENERAL ALBERT SIDNEY JOHNSTON,
UTAH EXPEDITION

—Courtesy of Henry E. Huntington Library.

THOMAS L. KANE, FRIEND OF THE MORMONS

shipped 500 revolvers. Carson Valley not only responded with 2,700 pounds of church and public ammunition, and a wagon load of guns, but had purchased another $800 worth of armament in San Francisco.

All through that hectic summer, fall and winter, Utah had seethed with preparation for war. Sugar House, southeast of Salt Lake City—in the factory building which had seen Mormondom's earliest attempts at manufactury of sugar from beets—a chemical laboratory had been established, and gunpowder produced in substantial quantities. On Temple Square a shop was erected and, reportedly under license from Samuel Colt, was soon turning out replicas of the famous Colt revolver at the rate of twenty per week. Other shops in Salt Lake City were manufacturing rifles, canister bombs, bullets, and cannon balls.

With arrival of one of the worst winters within Mormon recollection, it finally became apparent that the "enemy" at Camp Scott had no possible chance of reaching Salt Lake Valley, and could only freeze and fuss through the bitterly cold months ahead. Not until then did General Wells pull the bulk of his troops back closer to the city, leaving only alert guards to watch the winterbound canyon approaches. But, realizing at last that halting Johnston and his army was vastly different from defeating them, the hectic preparation for the inevitable spring offensive continued on unabated.

That fall and winter of 1857-1858 saw also the most drastic step of all in Brigham Young's mobilization plans—his abandonment of the Mormon colonies and outposts. This meant "calling home" all Saints through out America, and all missionaries from the east and overseas. Relinquishment and loss of Elk County Mission, Salmon River Mission, Carson Valley, and the thriving city of San Bernardino in California, were irreparable blows to the Church. Certainly the few hundred fighting men gained to Utah's garrison were scant recompense to the forfeiture of such precious and valuable real estate as Carson Valley and San Bernardino; to say nothing of the personal loss to the Saints in homes, businesses and family footholds. Property loss alone amounted to millions of dollars. The "Big Move," as the Mormons called it, proved a costly one.

It is ironic that the years previous to 1857 had been famine years in Utah. Only the fact that three annual seasons of crop failures, ending in 1856, had been followed by the bountiful harvest of 1857, could it have been possible to sustain the influx of citizenry from the abandoned colonies. The "Big Move" meant a frightening price to pay for the defense of Zion.

OMINOUS NEWS OUT OF WASHINGTON

But such determined resistance, the fiery reception given the Expedition's advancing units, and Utah's frantic and costly preparation for war, had not in any way intimidated Buchanan and the War Department. Contractors who were reaping fortunes in military freight to supply the Expedition, were frenziedly pushing for expansion of the Utah War. All these factors—the pugnacious attitude of the Mormons, War Department alacrity for the project, and civilian pressure for continuance of contractual profits, resulted now in the granting of congressional authority to call an additional 3,018 officers and men to the Utah Expedition—bringing the troop total engaged to 5,602.[4] General W. S. Harney was recalled to head this second expedition.

[4]*House Executive Documents,* No. 2, II, pp. 31-32. Circular from Army Headquarters to Chiefs of Staff.

Additional contracts were issued totalling close to $6,000,000 to cover costs for 4,500 wagons, 50,000 oxen, 4,000 mules, and 5,000 teamsters and attendants. The supply trains alone, starting west early in 1858 would, even when close-wheeled, extend over 50 miles — definitely a bit too big for effective punitive raids by Lot Smith and his mounted Saints. Contract for moving supplies for the Utah Expedition was given, without any attempt at open bidding for the prize, to the firm of Russell, Majors and Waddell. When these dealings became generally known throughout America, the Utah Expedition found itself suddenly re-named "the Contractors' War."

These ominous facts could not fail to drift over the Rockies to Brigham Young and his frantically contrived defense of the homeland. The Church tithing fund was tapped for all it would bear; Utah's territorial legislature, meeting in January, levied additional taxes to meet the mounting costs of hostilities. Another army of mounted riflemen, totalling 1,000 men, were equipped and fielded out of Church tithing. The estimated $1,000,000 for these additional troops put severest kind of strain on the Mormon sect and its people. Those who could not march off to meet the enemy, and who must remain behind to till the fields and mind the stores, were counseled by Church authorities to cache food against any eventualities—and to set torch to their properties, and "retreat to the mountain fastness" should Johnston's Army ever reach Zion.[5]

No matter how frantic the preparation, and how convincing and pugnacious the warlike rhetoric, there remained an uneasiness and fear among all the Mormon leaders, from Brigham Young down to the humblest of ward bishops. Exultance in the certainty that they had

[5]Roberts, *Comprehensive History*, vol. IV, p. 333.

forced America's military elite into starvation and freezing at Camp Scott was tempered in the gut-deep feeling that Washington's arousal to the grim facts was speeding overwhelming numbers of fresh troops westward. Already assembled were more wagons loaded with supplies than could be burned by ten times the raiders Utah could field. Saints at last were facing up to the grim possibility of eventual defeat.

For three days and three nights Brigham Young, the apostles, and others of the general authorities, fasted and prayed for God's help and favor in stemming the gathering tide against them; before retribution let loose, and the Valley be reddened with the blood of the Saints.[6] While Brigham Young, as governor, publicly thundered out in bellicose statements against Johnston's winterbound army, and the governmental interference into the lives of his people, there is ample evidence that he was desperately seeking an acceptable way out of the tangle. Everything in his power was now being directed toward preventing any Mormon incidents which might bring the troops into and through the canyons.

BUCHANAN AND KANE

And, while Johnston's Army shivered and fumed outside the gates, President Buchanan, and all of Washington, were suddenly finding themselves deluged with questions and angry criticism for this blundering and ill-conceived war on those strange religionists who had already fled to Utah in search of the peace denied them in Illinois and Missouri. Whether or not Brigham Young knew it, American sentiment was rapidly swinging in his favor.

[6]*Journal History*, Salt Lake City, entries of Feb. 21, 22, 23, 1858.

The press had mounted a campaign of scathing criticism against President Buchanan and his drastic adventure. Fair-minded editors, preachers, and politicians were suddenly extolling the Mormons and their gutty stand. "The Contractors' War" had become, and now was being criticized and denounced as "Buchanan's Blunder." The American president, smarting under ridicule and censure, had become as anxious for an honorable way out of his blunder as was Brigham Young in far away Utah.

Whether Thomas L. Kane was summoned by President Buchanan to aid in solving the pernicious dilemma, or whether Kane offered himself as secret mediator toward a peaceful solution of it, cannot be ascertained. There is no question but what Kane had been apprised through that anxious winter, by letters forwarded from Governor Young through Utah's congressional delegate John M. Bernhisel, concerning the problems being faced by the Saints in countering a military expedition "unjustly" thrown upon them. That Kane was one Gentile who could penetrate the vales of Zion, talk sensibly with his loyal friend Brigham, and perhaps somehow work out a compromise between the Mormon people and their government, was a fortuitous windfall eagerly seized upon by the worried and pressured Buchanan.

With presidential blessing, and probably with secret authority, Kane took ship from Boston to Panama, and crossed the isthmus by means of the new Panama Railroad, to Panama City on the Pacific side. And, at 3 p.m., Friday, January 15, 1848, Kane was aboard another steamship "moving smoothly out into the Pacific" and bound for San Francisco.[7]

[7]Winther, Oscar O. (ed.), *The Private Papers and Diary of Thomas Leiper Kane*, pp. 66-69.

Kane's diary indicates that he was making every possible endeavor to keep his identity secret. On the ship from New England to Panama, in crossing the isthmus aboard the railroad, and all the way to San Francisco he was registered and known as "A. Osborne, Botanist."

On January 29, 1858 Kane was in San Francisco. "Drove crazily about the strange streets hunting for Mormons," he confided to his journal, "two hours before I found one."[8] Most of San Francisco's Saints, he discovered, had already heeded the "big move" and had returned by way of San Pedro, San Bernardino, and thence by long haul to Salt Lake City by wagon and team.

A few days later Thomas L. Kane, still under the elaborate incognito of Dr. A. Osborne, was following the retreating Saints by taking passage from San Francisco south aboard the coastwise *Great Republic.* It proved a miserable, uncomfortable trip—a painful repetition of the endless miles he had already traveled by sea. After a needed rest in Los Angeles, he traveled sixty miles by horseback to the Mormon community of San Bernardino. The company of Saints he joined, in their return to Zion, had no idea but what they were hauling a distinguished botanist from Philadelphia to study and catalog the flora of the Great Basin, rather than the Colonel Kane who had visited the Mormon camps before their great removal to Salt Lake Valley.

Kane's trip from San Bernardino was a speedy one. By February 25, 1858, he was in Salt Lake City, and "Dr. A. Osborne, Botanist" was closeted with his old friend Brigham Young. The immense and strenuous journey, he insisted, was in the name of peace, and strictly on his own volition.

[8]*Ibid.*, p. 75.

In confidence, he found the Mormon leader a perturbed and worried man. To the world, and to his people, Brigham was denouncing the "invasion," and reiterating the promise to either repulse the enemy, or to leave Utah as barren and devoid of habitation as the Saints had found it a decade earlier. Hit-and-run resistance had stopped Johnston's Army cold at Utah's portals, but a long winter, and continuous bad news out of Washington, had made only too devastatingly apparent that eventual defeat in civil war was inevitable.

Utah's territorial governor could see nothing ahead but blood and suffering for the Saints. Quickly as the snow melted, United States troops, double in strength, amply reinforced, would begin storming the canyon passages. As head of the Church, Brigham, and his apostles, were already praying for some miracle to intervene that might allow peace with honor. It must have pleased the tortured leader that Colonel Kane, at immense suffering and sacrifice, had traveled half the world to bring—directly from Buchanan—at least a chance for that miracle.

The bargain, if indeed it was a bargain, was an hard one. For Brigham Young it meant a stepping down from the high seat of defiance; and a definite loss of face in the struggle for the Utah Saints. Two things which the American President had set in motion must be followed through to completion, because, by sheer momentum, they could not, at this late date, be reversed. First of all, Brigham Young was dismissed as territorial governor. Alfred Cumming, as presidential appointee, must be allowed to safely move himself and family from Camp Scott to Salt Lake City, and thereupon take up his new duties as head of the territory. Secondly, the troops of the United States must definitely enter; hopefully without bloodshed and resistance by the Utah defenders.

These hard terms meant defeat, and a biting of the bullet for the pugnacious Brigham. But apparently Kane had brought assurance that Buchanan had lost all stomach for an actual war in Utah; that the troops, if allowed peaceable entry, would not occupy Salt Lake City nor any other Mormon communities, and would not take vindictive revenge on the Mormons or their leaders. Apparently also there must have been mentioned the intention of the American President to appoint a committee of investigation of what now had become a national travesty; that Mormon cries of injustice would definitely no longer go unheeded.

Certainly an abrupt change occurred with Thomas L. Kane's appearance in Salt Lake City. Brigham, of course, stubbornly refused to consider the opening of Zion's gates to the "enemy," but he had no objection to Kane's offer to go to Camp Scott, bearing a letter to Governor-elect Cumming, inviting him to come to Salt Lake City, negotiate the hostilities, and even take up his duties as territorial head. Cumming's entry, however, must be peaceable and secure; and totally without U.S. military escort. Brigham Young was not yet ready to so graciously allow the same favor to Johnston and his troops.

On March 8, Colonel Kane, dropping all botanical pretense, started out through snowbound Echo Canyon toward Camp Scott. He was furnished Utah militia escort as far as Little Muddy, which was within twelve miles of the American military winter camp. From that point Kane proceeded alone. His arrival was duly noted by an *Atlantic Monthly* journalist attached to Johnston's Army:

"On the previous evening—March 12th—the monotony of the camp had been unexpectedly disturbed by the arrival, from the direction of Salt Lake City, of a horseman completely exhausted by the fatigue and cold, who proved to be no other than Mr. Kane, whose mission to the 'Mormons' by way of California was at that time totally unknown to the army. The next morning he introduced himself to the governor [Cumming], was received as his guest, and remained in conference with him throughout the day. What was the character of their communication is unknown, except by inference from its results."[9]

The fact that Kane was not immediately escorted to the army commander, rather than to a civilian dignitary sharing camp, would indicate that Kane was purposely ignoring General Johnston, and his military, or that Johnston was deliberately rejecting anything or anybody coming out of that nest of treason beyond the mountains. That Kane did experience some sort of unpleasant encounter with the army picket who challenged his entry would indicate either a chilly reception from the military, or deliberate rejection.

Tullidge claims that Kane ignored the challenge of the sentry at the first picket post encountered. The guard, receiving no satisfactory answer to his challenge, reputedly fired on Kane. The Colonel then "broke the stock of his rifle over the sentry's head . . . The shot and the tussle, bringing other soldiers, the visitor was quickly surrounded, whereby with characteristic politeness, as well as diplomacy, [Kane] requested to be conducted to the tent of Governor Cumming,"[10] which was done, and the governor reportedly received him with cordiality.

That the broken gun incident is recorded first by Tullidge, and remains unmentioned in more official documents and letters, makes it questionable as to accuracy. It

[9]"The Utah Expedition," *Atlantic Monthly,* April 1859, p. 479.

[10]Tullidge, Edward W., *Life of Brigham Young,* 1877, p. 292.

does not seem likely that Colonel Kane, with his background in military custom, politics, law, and diplomacy, would violate simple military precaution by blundering into an army camp, and raising enough turmoil at the sentry gate to land him into custody as an intruding enemy. But the fact that Johnston snubbed and avoided him for days, and what contact Kane made with the haughty commander was by letter alone, even within the camp, would indicate that there was some sort of altercation over Kane's right to enter Camp Scott. Doubtless there was solid suspicion on the part of the military that he was part of the common enemy, and should be treated as such.

KANE AT CAMP SCOTT

But Cumming was friendly and receptive, and the first days of Kane's historic visit at Camp Scott were spent in company with the new governor of the Territory of Utah.

Certainly Johnston had every right to view his presence with suspicion and defiance. No one from government circles in Washington had notified him that there was a man circulating through the camps of the enemy with any official right to negotiate peace or to alter governmental proposals as to conduct of this war. Johnston had only his orders from the commander-in-chief—to occupy Utah. Mormons had chosen to resist his entry, to fight the army under his command. He would put down the rebellion. When the passes were clear and negotiable, and quickly as the necessary supplies and reinforcements arrived, the Mormons would get the decisive arguments of shot and steel.

Kane's mission, though it primarily concerned the assumption to office of the presidential appointees, Governor Alfred Cumming and Chief Justice Delaney R.

Eckels, and contained nothing that could be construed as Mormon military overtures to Johnston and his army, he had come burdened with matters that at least rated discussion with the army commander. So long as Kane concerned himself with civil matters, even lengthy sessions with the territorial appointees, Johnston showed not the slightest hint of interest. It was when Kane started plying the aloof commander with camp-written letters, that he received those terse, negative notes that remained cold, authoritative and boorish on every question.

In vain Kane pleaded with Johnston to accept Brigham Young's gracious offer of beef and 20,000 pounds of flour to the suffering army. Johnston refused to concede that his army *was* suffering. Emphatically he rejected anything tendered by "enemies of the government," and reminded Kane that all intercourse with the enemy was prohibited by the 56th and 57th articles of war. And as to Johnston sharing conference with the new civil authorities and Mormon leaders or emissaries, and any hint of negotiating the imminent assault on Utah, were matters which he abruptly dismissed.

"However unfortunate the position now occupied by that portion of the citizens of Utah belonging to the sect of Mormons," Johnston answered, "it is of their own seeking, and it is one from which they can be relieved by the mere act of obedience to the proclamation of Governor Cumming. Having the question of peace or war under his own control, President Young would, should he choose the latter, be responsible for all consequences."[11]

During his sojourn at Camp Scott, Colonel Kane strove in every honorable way to persuade General Johnston to

[11]Johnston to Kane, April 15, 1858. *House Executive Documents,* 35th Congress, 2nd session, vol. II, pt. ii, p. 88. In the letter, Johnston asks Kane to communicate its text to Brigham Young.

THE UNITED STATES EXPEDITION TO UTAH

—From Stenhouse, *The Rocky Mountain Saints.*

enter negotiations with himself and the territorial officers in peaceful settlement of Utah affairs. He was rebuffed in camp as an alien undesirable by Johnston and the military, even while being accepted and respected by Governor Cumming and Chief Justice Eckels.

The commander's attitude toward Kane remained churlish and sarcastic; his answers to the peace emissary's notes were abrupt and antagonistic. Johnston was there to march into Utah, to put down rebellion, to punish Brigham Young and any and every Mormon who chose fighting rather than unconditional surrender. He had orders from the President and War Department to achieve that objective. In the absence of official word to the contrary, he would not, and could not, recognize any crackpot emissary coming to him via the circuitous route of the enemy stronghold, no matter how eloquent his plea, or how pretentious his claims.

The snobbish impasse was brought to dramatic climax by a strange and inexplicable act on the part of General Johnston. "An invitation to an officers' dinner was dispatched from headquarters to Colonel Kane — regarded by General Johnston's friends as in itself a great compliment in a camp where rations were so abridged. The orderly entrusted with the delivery of the invitation 'whether maliciously or not it does not appear,' says the *Atlantic Monthly* writer, 'pretended to have mistaken his directions and proceeded to place him [Kane] under arrest.' 'The mistake, when discovered,' continues the writer here followed, 'was of course immediately rectified.' Colonel Kane, however, was convinced that the arrest was a studied insult, and wrote a challenge to Colonel Johnston, and 'applied to a gentleman from Virginia to act as his second.' The gentleman declined to act, and Colonel Kane's action coming to the knowledge of Judge

Eckels, the latter informed Governor Cumming that he had ordered the United States marshal to arrest all the parties concerned, 'in case another step should be taken in the affair.' The *Atlantic Monthly* writer declares that it was not until some time afterwards that the transactions came to the knowledge of General Johnston."[12]

The real success of Kane's three-week stay in Camp Scott was his final persuasion of Governor Alfred Cumming to make the trip over the mountains to Salt Lake City, and trust to the people of Utah to receive him as their governor. Cumming readily and courageously accepted the Mormon stipulation that it would be without military escort. Kane was not nearly so successful in inducing Chief Justice Eckels to undertake the journey.

For Judge Eckels, by now, was deeply engrossed in setting up the "district court" spring term, Camp Scott, in Green River County. Already he had charged the camp's "grand jury" to be explicit in investigating the prevailing practice of polygamy. He cautioned the jury, in their scheduled study of the pernicious doctrine that: "It cannot be concealed, gentlemen, that certain domestic arrangements exist in this territory destructive of the peace, good order, and morals of society — arrangements at variance with those of all enlightened and Christian communities in the world; and sapping as they do the very foundations of all virtue, honesty, and morality. It is an imperative duty falling upon you as grand jurors diligently to inquire into this evil and make every effort to check its growth . . . "[13]

[12]Roberts, *Comprehensive History*, vol. IV, pp. 355-356. For the quotations from *Atlantic Monthly*, see issue of April 1859, p. 481.

[13]The full charge of Judge Eckels was published in *Atlantic Monthly*, April 1959, pp. 481-482.

The fact that Judge Eckels' grand jury and "district court" had to function far removed from the action, is probably the reason they failed to come up with any specific indictments of functioning polygamists. But Eckels did succeed in bringing indictments against Brigham Young and a select list of Mormon John Does, on the handier and less complex charge of treason.

The court, which to the military had been farcical and comical from the start, possessed a far greater drawback to Colonel Kane. It had prevented the territory's Chief Justice from moving with Cumming into Salt Lake City where be belonged. Yet, in spite of this setback, Governor Cumming had been persuaded to meet the people he was to govern face to face. In itself this was one pleasing indication that the weeks at Camp Scott had not been in vain.

So, on March 28, 1858, Kane could record in his diary: "I have returned from a trip [to the governor's headquarters] on which I was *successful* in making the arrangements for *introducing Governor C. [Cumming]* into the Valley, with the feeling that I have now done my last utmost, and may leave the future to a less finite Power."[14]

[14]Winther, Oscar O. (ed.), *The Private Papers and Diary of Thomas Leiper Kane*, p. 77.

"ROCKY MOUNTAIN MISERIES"
FOR UTAH EXPEDITION
— From *Harper's Weekly*, April 24, 1858.

X

"*Burn the Cities . . . Lay the Country Waste*"

BACK in Salt Lake City, and especially during the weeks of Kane's sojourn at Camp Scott, drastic changes were under way. Kane's earliest talks with Brigham Young had brought only willingness on the part of the Mormon leader to gracefully accept deposition as governor of Utah Territory, and for Cumming and the other presidential civil appointees to enter Salt Lake City to take up their duties, unchallenged, and in perfect safety.

Kane had not been nearly so successful in curbing Brigham's anger, distrust, and resolve to resist Buchanan, Johnston, and the great army that now extended like a sinuous snake all the way across the plains—its rattling tail at Fort Leavenworth; its fanged and poisonous head at Camp Scott. "I will say, in reference to Pres. Buchanan," Brigham declared, "that for his outrageous wicked ness in this movement he shall wear the yoke as long as he lives; he shall be led about by his party with the yoke on his neck . . . and his name shall be forgotten."[1]

[1]*Journal History*, Church Historian's Office, Salt Lake City, entry of Sept. 6, 1857.

Though Colonel Kane had gone to Camp Scott fully cognizant of Brigham Young's implacable antipathy toward Johnston's "invasion" of the peaceful and struggling Mormon Zion, he'd left a lot from his earnest and persuasive talks for the Mormon leader to mull over. And his sincerity, and willingness to brave cold and physical peril to promote a peaceful end to a military blumder as embarrassing to the American government as it was to the Mormon people, had laid an honest pattern, whereby both Brigham and Johnston could still honorably wriggle off their twin peaks of fury. He was bringing Governor Cumming into Salt Lake City—even though he now personally despaired of ever averting the bloody fighting so inevitably ahead.

On March 18, while Kane was sojourning at Camp Scott, Brigham Young, acting as president of his Church, had called a "Council of War." Attendant were the full first presidency, the twelve apostles, and officers of the Nauvoo Legion. Out of this "Council of War" had come a new and dramatic decision—a complete reversal of strategy—the total abandonment of armed resistance to Johnston's Army. "President Young's plan was to go into the desert and not war with the people [of the United States], but [to] let them destroy themselves."[2] "Move south!" was now the cry.

At the meeting in the tabernacle, the following Sunday, before which the Council's decisions were placed, the temper of the Saints of Utah showed marked difference from previous assemblages. The regular Sabbath service, converted in the crisis to a special conference, indicated sudden willingness to accept flight rather than fight.

President Young "spoke of the situation of affairs at this crisis and presented the policy which he intended to

[2]*History of Brigham Young, MS.*, 1858, p. 266.

pursue, which was to remove the grain and the women and children from the city and then, if needs be, burn it and lay the country waste."[3]

The Saints were to flee their homes, their farms, their cities, and remove themselves to the southern deserts. If the invading troops molested one person, one dwelling, in Salt Lake City or elsewhere, every community, house and farm in Utah would be torched, and fire and ruin would wipe away every vestige of Mormon occupation. The United States Army would get a Utah as bare of growth and habitation as the Saints themselves had found it ten years previous. Though an harsh and emphatic decree, the Mormon people, in conference assembled, received it willingly, and without dissent.

"Rather than see my wives and daughters ravished and polluted, and the seeds of corruption sown in the hearts of my sons by a brutal soldiery, I would leave my home in ashes, my gardens and orchards a waste, and subsist upon roots and herbs, a wanderer through these mountains for the remainder of my natural life."[4] Brigham Young had already made this amply plain, long before the decision for the "big move." Destruction of the settlements, and flight, had from the first been coupled with Mormon battle strategy should Johnston succeed in fighting his way into the valley. But the new mood, with decisive immediacy, was to abandon all without first resisting the "invaders."

Even though the conference had "sustained" this sacrificial course of action, there is evidence that the decision was not universally popular throughout all the territory. It took some urging, preaching and publicity to get the

[3]*Ibid.*, entry for Sunday, Mar. 21, 1858, pp. 269-272.

[4]Letter quoted in West, Ray B. Jr., *Kingdom of the Saints* (New York, 1957), p. 263.

proposal into full accord. And too, many "Gentile" merchants of Salt Lake City, anxious for trading with the enemy, had looked forward to conducting business with the U.S. troops in something other than burned-out store buildings.

". . . On the 21st inst. [March], it was unanimously agreed to abandon 'Sebastopol' to our enemies, without the consent of Lord Raglan, if they persist in carrying out the unconstitutional policy adopted by the present [Buchanan] administration."[5] The historical allusion in this declaration of intent to flee and destroy is made clear when one considers the official dispatch of the Russian general who had only recently evacuated Sebastopol: "It is not Sebastopol which we have left to them [the conquerors], but the burning ruins of the town, which we ourselves set fire to, having maintained the honor of defense in such a manner that our grandchildren may recall with pride the remembrance of it, and send it on to all posterity. . . .The Russians had made of Sebastopol another Moscow."[6]

If, by this act, Brigham Young wanted posterity's remembrance of it, the shrewd and resourceful leader was to succeed beyond his wildest dream. Out of such dramatic acts come the remembered high peaks of history.

Wagons, piled high with family belongings, began moving southward toward the rim towns of the southern deserts and Utah's "Dixie." On April 8 an express arrived in the half-deserted Salt Lake City with information that Governor Alfred Cumming and Colonel Thomas L. Kane were on their way into Zion, without guard or United States military trappings.

[5]See Roberts, *Comprehensive History,* vol. IV, pp. 364-365.
[6]McCarthy, Justin, History of Our Own Times, Am. Ed., vol. II, pp. 264-265.

Mormon militia met the party at the head of Echo Canyon, presented arms, and bade the new governor a welcome to Utah. By night, and by light of huge bonfires, he was escorted through the canyon. Repeatedly he was challenged by sentries and troops; repeatedly he delivered his firelight speech responsive to the welcome. Actually the whole performance was something of an imposition on Cumming's good nature. After each ritual the same party of Mormons would slip ahead through the darkness, challenge the governor, and repeat the ceremony. Cumming was amazed at the number of Utah troops, and their alertness in guarding Zion's portals.

The carriage ride through Weber Canyon took another day. At its mouth Cumming was met by uniformed detachments of militia. The official party was escorted to Farmington courthouse, where a Mormon band played "The Star Spangled Banner," and the new governor made yet another speech.

On the main road into Salt Lake City, Cumming began meeting hundreds of Mormon evacuees fleeing southward. At Hot Springs, north of Utah's territorial capital, his party was joined by the city's mayor, aldermen and councilmen, as escort to comfortable quarters in the city of the fleeing Saints.

Preliminary conferences with Brigham Young and leading rebels were so completely amicable that Cumming could write a little exultantly to Johnston: "I have been everywhere recognized as the governor of Utah; and so far from having encountered insults and indignities, I am gratified in being able to state to you that in passing through the settlements, I have been universally greeted with such respectful attention as are due to the representative of the executive authority of the United States in the territory."[7]

[7]*House Executive Documents*, 35th Congress, 2nd session, II, pt.ii, 72-73.

Mormons, however, continued without pause in their evacuation of the cities. Of this Cumming was puzzled and unhappy. Yet his conferences with church leaders were frequent and fruitful. Every opportunity was extended him to examine territorial court records. Everything, he found, including the library, was intact, and not burned as reported. The Secretary's safe had been cached in a privy to save it, in case the city burned. Its contents had not been molested.

Cumming's report to the United States Secretary of State was that every record and document was "perfect and unimpaired."[8]

On April 25 Governor Cumming addressed the remaining Mormons, in the tabernacle. Fervidly he pleaded with them to return to their homes. But, since he was unable to promise that Johnston's Army would not enter, his pleadings were totally without avail. Utah's evacuation continued.

On May 13, in desperate attempt to dissuade Johnston from making final entry, Cumming and Kane hurried back to Camp Scott. Johnston, however, had clearly made up his mind. Quickly as reinforcements arrived he would commence his military campaign in Utah. Cumming, now completely on the side of the desperate Saints, hauled wife and family back to Salt Lake City. Despite every obstacle, it was his full and declared intent to honorably fulfill the role of territorial governor.

As for Thomas L. Kane, he was of the opinion he had done all in his power to solve the crisis. From Camp Scott he returned to the east, overland by way of Florence, Nebraska. He was glad to avail himself of Mormon escort.

[8]*Ibid.*, pp. 93-94.

XI

"*When Johnston's Army Comes . . . !*"

IN THE unpredictable fashion of American democracy, public opinion in the east had by now undergone radical change. Buchanan was under intense fire from both Congress and the press. Graft of the army contractors had provoked congressional investigation. The dramatic evacuation of the Mormon people had caught public fancy. Brigham Young, instead of being the world's most obscene rascal, was suddenly being lauded by the press as another Prince of Orange, and a hero.

The *New York Daily Times* had already come out critically against "Buchanan's blunder," and in support of the Mormons and their stand. "This action strikes us as being much more hasty than wise. It is like most anti-Mormon movements—the result of impulse rather than good policy or common sense. It would puzzle ordinary men, we suspect, to explain why a hostile army was sent against Utah at the outset. There were undoubted disorders in the affairs of the territory; but it has never yet been shown that they were such as could be remedied by fire and sword. . . .The whole Utah business has been mismanaged in the most extraordinary manner from the beginning; and if it does not end in open and bloody rebellion, it is not likely to be saved from that issue by any special wisdom on the part of the general government."[1]

President Buchanan now well knew what is was to "wear the yoke." All through that winter stalemate, with help of a willing press, the public became increasingly aroused over his presumptuous flinging of the army against Utah without previously ascertaining the facts of the alleged rebellion.

Senator Sam Houston, of Texas, politically sensitive to the military adventure, answered the War Department's request for more money and more troops for the Utah Expedition: "If they [the Mormons] have to be subdued—and God defend us from such a result—and the valley of Salt Lake is to be ensanguined with the blood of American citizens, I think it will be one of the most fearful calamities that has befallen this country . . . I deprecate it as an intolerable evil. I am satisfied that the executive has not had the information he ought to have had on the subject before making such movement as he had directed to be made. I am convinced that facts have been concealed from him. I think his wisdom and patriotism should have dictated the propriety of ascertaining, in the first place, whether the people of Utah were willing to submit to the authority of the United States.

"Why not send to them men to whom they could unbosom themselves, and see whether they would say, 'We are ready to submit to the authorities of the United States, if you send us honest men and gentlemen, whose morals, whose wisdom, and whose character, comport with the high station they fill; we will surrender to them; we will

[1]*New York Daily Times*, issue of Dec. 24, 1857.

give up our [political] authority, and act in obedience to the laws of the United States.' If this course had been taken by the executive, I am sure he would never have recommended war; and if the fact had been before the secretary of war, I am sure he never would have made the recommendation which he has submitted to us."[2]

President Buchanan was politician enough to recognize the imperative necessity of saving face. While American troops fretted and froze at Camp Scott, he grasped at every opportunity to squirm off the skewer upon which he was being publicly and politically roasted. Urged by Utah's territorial representative, John M. Bernhisel, he had accepted the good offices of Thomas L. Kane. Kane's visit with the enemy, and his accomplishment in the name of peace, were more than gratifying to the worried president. And, in his choice of Albert Cumming to replace Brigham Young as Utah's territorial governor, he had fortuitously enlisted a man of high principles; a man who had risen above political vindictiveness in his honest effort to serve Utah and his nation.

Gratifying as were these twin developments, James Buchanan still was a long way from winning back public confidence and approval for the military and juridical blunders of the Utah War. In urgent and abrupt about-face, the president appointed a "Peace Commission," composed of L.W. Powell, former governor of Kentucky, and Major Ben McCulloch, military hero from Texas. To these men, and for the Mormon people, President Buchanan entrusted a personally-signed "proclamation of pardon." On May 29, 1858, after a frantic express trip across the plains, Powell and McCulloch arrived at Camp Scott.

[2]*Congressional Globe,* Feb. 25, 1858. 35th Congress, 1st session, pt. i, pp. 873-874.

ALBERT SIDNEY JOHNSTON, AGE 57
Engraved from a Photograph Taken in
Salt Lake City in 1869

—From *Century Magazine*, Vol. XXIX, 1884.

Johnston, as commander of the military, was dumfounded. His orders had been to enter Utah; to subdue the rebellion. The orders had been clearly made, and never rescinded—not even by a vacillating commander-in-chief. Now, before the Mormon rebels had deservedly felt the army's steel, political meddling had intruded itself into the campaign. Johnston understandably stormed in fury over the incredible appearance of Powell and McCulloch, bearing sweeping presidential pardon to every blackhearted and traitorous Mormon who had any hand in the act.

Leaving behind them an angry American general at Camp Scott, the Peace Commission took off for Salt Lake City. They arrived there June 7, 1858, to find the place deserted and readied for the torch. It was necessary for them to petition the Church leaders, who were at Fillmore and settlements far to the south, requesting their return to Salt Lake City for conference. After a reluctant and cagey Brigham Young and apostles arrived back in the city, they were joined by Governor Cumming, and talks were started in the boarded-up Council House.

THE ARMY MOVES ON ZION

But for Albert Sidney Johnston, the die was cast, the season was late. No vacillating government nor politically-frightened president was going to dissuade him from starting his troops on the last leg of this campaign. So it was that, in midst of their talks for peace, the Commissioners and Governor were amazed and embarrassed to hear that the army was on the move.

Frantically they endeavored to convince Brigham and the Saints it just could not be so; that it would be highly irregular, and a malfeasance of duty for Johnston to give such orders. But Governor Cumming's frantic appeal and rebuke to the commander were ignored. Johnston had broken up Camp Scott; all the vast military settlement around Fort Bridger. At long last the army was on the march; and in no mood to halt.

The *Atlantic Monthly,* through its correspondent, preserves a visual record of the demise of Camp Scott: "On the 13th day of June, the long camp was broken up, the army moved forward in three columns on the route through the canons. Although the season was so far advanced, snow had fallen at the fort only three days before. The streams were swollen and turbulent with spring floods, and difficulty was anticipated in crossing the Bear and Weber rivers. Material for bridging had, therefore, been prepared, and accompanied the first column.

"Southwest of the fort, at the distance of four or five miles, a singular *butte,* the top of which is as level as the floor of a ballroom, rises to the heights of eight hundred feet above the valley's Black Fork, and commands a view of the entire broad plateau between Wind River and the Uintah and Wasatch ranges. Little parties of horsemen could be seen spurring up the gullies on its almost precipitous sides, to witness from its summit the departure of the army. The scene was in the highest degree picturesque. Almost at their feet lay the camp, the few tents which remained unstruck glittering like bright dots on the wing of an insect; the whitewashed wall of the fort [Bridger] reflecting the sunshine, while stacks of turf chimneys, lodge poles, and rubbish, marked the spots where the encampment had been abandoned.

"The whole valley was in commotion. Along the strips of road were winding clumsy baggage trains the regiment of dragoons was trailing in advance; the gleam of musket-barrels of the infantry was visible on all sides; and every puff of the breeze that blew over the bluff was freighted with the rumble of artillery carriages and caissons. Here and there were groups of half-naked Indians galloping to and fro, with fluttering blankets, gazing at the show with the curiosity and delight of children."[3]

Once more the troops were on the move. And the common soldier, unaware of politics, peace commissions, or even the true heart of the enemy they at least were getting a chance to fight, whooped and sang for the sheer joy of being freed from the miseries of Camp Scott.

"The Mormons knew that Uncle Sam
Had troops upon the route,
And Brigham prayed the Holy Lamb
Would help to clean them out.
"The distance then, one thousand miles,
Me in the face did stare,
For Brigham swore no damned gentiles
Again should winter there.[4]

Even though the great army had started moving, the Saints now made no attempt to intercept it. Lot Smith and his flying horsemen remained totally behind Zion's barricades. There were no nightly harassments of the troops; no torches; no billowing smoke; no burned-out wagons. Nor had orders gone out for the long expected pitched battle at Echo Canyon. While Johnston's Army moved upon them, Mormons were hearing out the Peace Commission's frantic attempts to pardon them before the troops could enter Zion.

A PEACE, FRANTICALLY OFFERED

The Peace Commission had come to Salt Lake City fortified with every device to secure the peace—save one—the inability to hold the U.S. expeditionary forces at

[3]*Atlantic Monthly*, for April 1859. See also Roberts, *Comprehensive History*, vol. IV, p. 444.

[4]*The Puts Songster*, published by D.E. Appleton & Co. in various editions during the 1850s.

Camp Scott until their mission could be accomplished. While the proclamation of President Buchanan to the people of Utah listed the alleged crimes of Mormondom for the historical record, it was immeasurably conciliatory toward any and all perpetrators of such depravity.

"Now, therefore, I James Buchanan, president of the United States," the instrument concluded, "have thought proper to issue this, my *proclamation*, enjoining upon all public officers of the territory of Utah, to be diligent and faithful, to the full extent of their power, in the execution of their laws; commanding all citizens of the United States in said territory, to aid and assist the officers in the performance of their duties; offering to the inhabitants of Utah, who shall submit to the laws, a free pardon for the seditions and treason heretofore by them committed; warning those who shall persist, after notice of this proclamation in the present rebellion against the United States, that they must expect no further lenity . . ."[5]

The Saints, however, even while Johnston's Army moved ever closer toward Salt Lake City, remained stubbornly insistent they were guilty of no wrong-doing.

Powell and McCulloch were desperately anxious to hang the cloak of probity and sanctity on Brigham and the apostles, and get the hell out of Utah before there could be any possibility of bloodshed. In the church Council House, the windows boarded up, and the glass removed to safe-keeping before the expected torching, the Peace Commissioners listened to the biting oratory of Apostle George Albert Smith in Zion's verbal defense. However, after fidgeting through days of forensic purgings by Mormon leaders—to their hysterical anger against the politicians who had falsely accused them, and had thrown an army against them as participants in a rebellion that al-

[5]*Messages and Papers of the Presidents,* vol. V, pp. 493-495.

ways had been a myth hatched in Washington—the Mormons finally agreed to a compromise. They would accept guilt only for burning of the supply trains. So, with a sigh of relief, the commissioners quickly and unconditionally pardoned them for even this wrong.

Remainder of the presidential cake was generously left on the table, to be eaten or rejected, as the Saints might feel inclined. And then Brigham Young himself suddenly and amicably bowed to circumstance.

Since the earlier presidential decree that the army must enter Utah had somehow failed to be rescinded by the pardon, it was apparent that time and necessity left no choice. Brigham, therefore, would allow the army to enter Salt Lake City—but *under no circumstances* must Johnston halt his troops. Buchanan's political promises could thus be kept. The president would save face by the army's entry into the city. And even Johnston should be satisfied. But the promise was conditional to a pledge that troops march *through* Salt Lake City, and out again. Should the army halt, Mormons definitely would burn Zion to the earth.

The commissioners were satisfied. Everyone, including the Saints, could claim some sort of victory. As a sort of dessert to this feast of goodwill, and urged by an express message dispatched by Governor Cumming, even Johnston unbent enough to speed ahead of his troops a proclamation to the Saints:

> I . . . assure those citizens of the territory who, I learn, apprehend from the army ill treatment, that no person whatever will be in any wise interfered with or molested in his person or rights, or in the peaceful pursuit of his avocations; and, should protection be needed, that they will find the army (always faithful to the obligations of duty) as ready now to assist and protect them as it was to oppose them while it was believed they were resisting the laws of their government."[6]

protect them as it was to oppose them while it was believed they were resisting the laws of their government."[6]

In addition Johnston promised both Saints and commissioners that he would, on the day of arrival, encamp "beyond the Jordan." But still the wary Mormons made no move to return to their homes.

THE ENEMY IS HERE

On June 26, 1858, the great army entered a strange and silent city. To the stillness of almost utter desertion, broken only by the gurgle of City Creek, the army had its day of entry and exit.

"It was one of the most extraordinary scenes that has occurred in American history. All day long, from dawn until sunset, the troops and trains poured through the city, the utter silence of the streets being broken only by the music of the military bands, the monotonous tramp of the regiments, and the rattle of the baggage wagons. The numerous flags, which had been flying from staffs on the public buildings during the previous week, were all struck. The only visible groups of spectators were on the corners near Brigham Young's residence, and consisted almost entirely of Gentile civilians."[7]

Albert Sidney Johnston, able campaigner, had so arranged the previous day's march as to enter Salt Lake Valley through Emigration Canyon at dawn. This allowed a full day for the march to the promised stopping point west of the Jordan River, and avoiding any necessity for encampment within the city limits. There was no doubt in anyone's mind that Mormons would execute

[6]House Executive Documents, 35th Congress, 2nd sess., II, pt. 11, pp. 119-121.

[7]*Atlantic Monthly*, April 1859, p. 490.

JOHNSTON'S ARMY "INVADES" SALT LAKE CITY

—From Stenhouse, *The Rocky Mountain Saints.*

MARKER AT SITE OF FORT BRIDGER
AND CAMP SCOTT
Erected in 1914

their "Sebastopol plan" at least infraction of the promise not to pause in the City of the Saints.

As the columns moved through, the military command found the city deserted, except for those few Mormon guards left to monitor the passage of the troops, and to lay the torch if necessity dictated. Choosing also to remain were a number of Gentile civilians and merchants who looked to the army as an economic windfall rather than a Mormon calamity. Official records show that the historic traverse of Salt Lake City was accomplished in the following order:

> (1) Brevet Colonel C. F. Smith's battalion, constituting the advance guard;
> (2) Tenth infantry and Phelps' battery;
> (3) Fifth infantry and Reno's battery;
> (4) Colonel Loring's battalion of mounted riflemen;
> (5) Volunteers;
> (6) Colonel Cooke's second dragoons, constituting the rear guard;
> Each command was followed by its train and a portion of the [main] supply train;
> The headquarters were with the advance.[8]

As the great army moved along South Temple Street, and westward out through the city, the Peace Commissioners, observant but satisfied, rode with the general's staff. Governor Alfred Cumming watched, unsure and nervous, from the window of his official residence along the march.

Colonel Philip St. George Cooke, now commanding the 2nd Dragoons in the U.S. Army, rode through Salt Lake City with head bared, and cap at breast—in deference to the courageous Mormon Battalion he had com-

[8]General Orders No. 30, House Executive Documents, 35th Congress, 2nd session, vol. II, p. 119. Also Report of General Johnston to Army Headquarters, June 28, from camp "near Salt Lake City," *Ibid.*, p. 121.

manded in the Mexican War. He hadn't forgotten those Mormons who, under his leadership, had marched from Council Bluffs to Fort Leavenworth, and thence across the deserts to California—a remarkable feat, and reputed to be the longest infantry march in history. As a fighting man he had learned, through trials and hardship of that war, to respect the sober and dependable Saints.

As to General Albert Sidney Johnston, he meticulously kept his pledge. The ranks went through unbroken. And the army never stopped moving until it was encamped in Cedar Valley, thirty-six miles from the City of the Saints.

CAMP FLOYD

Johnston's military rendezvous in Utah was to flower into the more permanent Camp Floyd. Other than an historical marker, nothing remains today of the great military base that for years would flourish as both gain and loss for the Mormons.

Gradually the Saints returned from the far south, to take up again their lives in Salt Lake City and the northern settlements. Alfred Cumming served Utah Territory as a capable, fair-minded, and wholly acceptable governor. And, still wondering what they had done to warrant military invasion and occupation, the Mormons once more settled in to the task of building Zion in a land which even the American bison had rejected.

But the ever resourceful Saints were not long in discovering that, by supplying the needs of Camp Floyd, they could reap solid profit in the sale of food to the huge garrison. Hay and grain were needed for Floyd's thousands of draft horses and cavalry mounts. And Mormons too discovered the contractors' usury always present in the handling of government freight. Zion's loss was mainly in the Gentile swarm who descended on Salt Lake

City; horny, drinking, fun-loving men whose morals and religious outlook never ceased to be outrageous to the straitlaced Saints.

Of the illustrious military commanders and officers who were instrumental in setting up Camp Floyd in Cedar Valley, the greater number of them were soon destined to be recalled east again to take up military tasks far more grim than "Buchanan's blunder" in the Utah wilderness. In the army which marched through Salt Lake City on that historic June day in 1858, was borne a roster of military elite who in a few years would be fighting on both sides of America's greater War Between the States. Some would rise to immortal stature in the mighty struggle. Others, like General Albert Sidney Johnston, would bravely die in advancing the rebel cause of the Confederates.

Though Camp Floyd continued for years as a bayonet in the flesh of the Saints, most of the original Utah Expedition, those who founded the camp, were eventually swallowed up in the blood and strife of America's imminent and more terrible conflict. Actually, everyone involved in the Utah War were, in one way or another, losers for it. Buchanan tumbled into political oblivion. Johnston and his army bled and died in the most fearful type of struggle. Mormons lost their California, Idaho and Nevada colonies—along with their precious insularity in the Far West.

So Johnston's Army came. Its troopers were neither "drowned in the lake," nor were their "bones left to bleach upon the sand." There continued to remain a lot of holy smoke in Utah, but it came not from burning wagons, nor from burning homes. Left at last to the inexorable breezes of time, all this eventually blew away. And, wafted finally into forgetful silence, slowly went each and every bitter memory of the Utah War.

BIBLIOGRAPHY

BIBLIOGRAPHY

GENERAL SOURCES

Acts, Resolutions and Memorials. Passed at the several sessions of the Legislative Assembly of the Territory of Utah from 1850-1861. Salt Lake City: 1855, 1866, 1870.

Arrington, Leonard J. *Great Basin Kingdom.* An Economic History of the Latter-day Saints, 1830-1900. Cambridge: Harvard University Press; 1958.

Bailey, Paul. *The Armies of God.* The Mormon Militia on the American Frontier. New York: Doubleday & Company; 1968.

______. *Jacob Hamblin, Buckskin Apostle.* Los Angeles: Westernlore Publishers; 1948; 1955; 1961. Salt Lake City: Bookcraft, Inc.; 1961; 1965.

______. "The Utah War," *Westerners Brand Book.* Los Angeles: Los Angeles Corral of Westerners; 1948.

Bancroft, Hubert H. *History of Utah.* San Francisco: The History Company; 1890.

Burton, Richard F. *The City of the Saints.* New York: Harper & Brothers, Publishers; 1862.

Cooke, Col. P. St. George. *Conquest of New Mexico and California.* The March of the Mormon Battalion. New York: G. P. Putnam & Sons; 1878.

Creer, Leland Hargrave. *The Founding of an Empire.* The Exploration and Colonization of Utah, 1776-1856. Salt Lake City: Bookcraft, Inc.: 1947.

Doctrine and Convenants of the Church of Jesus Christ of Latter-day Saints, containing Revelations Given to Joseph Smith, the Prophet. Salt Lake City: 1948 edition.

Egan, Howard. *Pioneering the West, 1846 to 1878.* Major Howard Egan's Diary. Richmond, Utah: Howard R. Egan Estate; 1917.

Gates, Susan Young, and Leah D. Widtsoe. *The Life Story of Brigham Young.* New York: Macmillan Company; 1931.

Golder, Frank Alfred. *The March of the Mormon Battalion.* New York: The Century Company; 1928.

Gove, Captain Jesse A. *The Utah Expedition; Letters of Captain Gove to Mrs. Gove and the New York Herald.* Concord, N.H.: New Hampshire Historical Society; 1928.

Hafen, LeRoy R. and Ann W. (Eds.). *The Utah Expedition, 1857-1858.* Far West and Rockies Series, vol. VIII. Glendale, Calif.: The Arthur H. Clark Company; 1958.

Hickman, William A. *Brigham's Destroying Angel.* New York: George A. Crofutt & Company; 1872. Salt Lake City: 1904.

House Executive Documents, 35th Congress, 1st and 2nd Sessions. Washington, D.C.: 1857; 1858.

Jenson, Andrew. *Church Chronology.* Salt Lake City: Deseret News Press; 1899.

Kane Thomas L. (Winther, Oscar Osburn, ed.) *A Friend of the Mormons.* The private papers and diary of Thomas Leiper Kane. San Francisco: Gelber-Lilienthal, Inc.; 1937.

______. *The Mormons.* New York: Macmillan Company; 1902. Reprinted 1923.

Linn, William A. *A Story of the Mormons.* New York: Macmillan Company; 1902. Reprinted 1923.

Little, James A. *From Kirtland to Salt Lake City.* Salt Lake City: Juvenile Instructor Office; 1890.

Lyford, Rev. C. P. *The Mormon Problem.* New York: Phillips & Hunt; 1886.

McGavin, E. Cecil. *U.S. Soldiers Invade Utah.* Boston: Meador Publishing Company; 1937.

O'Dea, Thomas F. *The Mormons.* Chicago: University of Chicago Press; 1957.

Remy, Jules and Brenchley, Julius. *A Journey to Great Salt Lake City.* Two vols. London; 1861.

Roberts, B. H. (author and editor). *Comprehensive History of the Church of Jesus Christ of Latter-day Saints.* Six vols. Salt Lake City: Deseret News Press; 1930.

______. *Outlines of Ecclesiastical History.* Salt Lake City: George Q. Cannon & Sons Co.; 1895.

Schindler, Harold. *Orrin Porter Rockwell, Man of God, Son of Thunder.* Salt Lake City: University of Utah Press; 1966.

Smith, Joseph (Roberts, B. H., ed.). *History of the Church,* Period I. Four vols. Salt Lake City: Deseret News Press, 1902.

Spencer, Clarissa Young, with Harmer, Mabel. *One Who Was Valiant.* A biography of Brigham Young. Caldwell, Idaho: The Caxton Printers, Ltd.; 1937.

Stenhouse, Thomas H. B. *Rocky Mountain Saints.* New York. D. Appleton & Company; 1873.

Tullidge, Edward W. *History of Salt Lake City.* Salt Lake City: 1886.

______. *History of Utah.* Two vols. Salt Lake City; 1889.

______. *Life of Brigham Young.* New York: 1876.

Waite, Mrs. C. V. *The Mormon Prophet and His Harem; or An Authentic History of Brigham Young, His Numerous Wives and Children.* Cambridge: 1866.

Werner, Morris R. *Brigham Young.* New York: Harcourt Brace & Company, Inc.; 1924.

West, Roy B. Jr. *Kingdom of the Saints.* New York; 1957.

Whitney, Orson F. *History of Utah.* Four vols. Salt Lake City: Deseret News Press; 1892.

Young, Brigham. *Journal of Discourses.* 26 vols. Liverpool and London: 1854-1886.

PERIODICALS

Atlantic Monthly. Issue of April 1859.

Congressional Globe. (Containing the debates and proceedings of Congress.) 28th to 35th Congress. Washington: 1854-1861.

Contributor, The. Salt Lake City. Monthly from 1878-1890. Vol. IX, from Nov. 1887 to Oct. 1888 contains much valuable information on the Nauvoo Legion and the Utah War, as recorded by R. W. Young.

Deseret News. Salt Lake City; 1852 to present.

Latter-day Saint Millennial Star. Liverpool, England. 1840 to present.

Morgan, Dale L. "The Sate of Deseret," *Utah Historical Quarterly,* VIII, Nos. 2-4. Salt Lake City: 1940.

Tracy, Captain Albert. "Journal of Captain Albert Tracy." *Utah Historical Quarterly,* XIII, 1-119; 1945.

MANUSCRIPTS

History of Brigham Young, MS., 1844-1877. Salt Lake City: Office of the Church Historian. Reproduced by photomechanical process from microfilm of original.

Journal History. L.D.S. Church Historian's Office, Salt Lake City. A day-to-day manuscript history of the Latter-day Saints, from the Church's inception to the present.

INDEX

INDEX

WESTERNLORE
BOOKS